More New England Graveside Tales

T. M. Gray

Schiffer Publishing Ltd®

4880 Lower Valley Road, Atglen, Pennsylvania 19310

Dedication

For my mother, with love.

Acknowledgments

No one ever writes a book alone. First, I must thank my family for their continued support, not only in my undertaking of *this* book, but the others as well. You guys are the best and I love you all.

To my pals who understood when I couldn't come out to play, chained to my desk by a demanding muse, who refused to let me *not* write. Thank you for your patience and love.

To everyone who shared their photos and art, and to the artists of old, a million thanks.

To those of the past who left a bread crumb trail of clues to follow up on, as well as those alive today who work to cover the many strange and fascinating topics, I wholeheartedly thank you.

To my fine editor, Dinah Roseberry and all the crew at Schiffer Books, many, many thanks.

Special thanks to Obsidian Dawn for use of the brushes.

And to my wonderful readers, those who take the time to write and tell me of their experiences with the unknown, as well as those who don't write but read my stuff, I can't thank you enough. This book is for you.

Author Note

There is so much to see in New England, but I've done my best to provide some interesting tidbits of history along the way and help in terms of directions, phone numbers, events, schedules, and admission fees. The admissions and tour tickets in this book reflect prices as they were upon publication. This information is provided only to aid the traveler with his/her budget planning. Prices in every establishment are liable to change at any given time, as are the days and hours of operation. It's always best to call ahead, or at the very least, check the website of where you plan to visit *before* you leave. Please keep in mind that phone numbers and website URLs may change over time. What doesn't change, however, is New England's fascinating history and the many locations to explore.

Most of the locations mentioned in this book are open to the public, however one should be careful not to trespass on private property or public areas that are closed. Not only is trespassing illegal; it can be dangerous as well. Always obtain the owner's permission before entering a posted area, and remember that most cemeteries are closed at night because of vandalism.

Always be mindful of your surroundings and leave an area exactly as you found it. Many museums prohibit the use of flash photography because it accelerates the deterioration of delicate artifacts and paintings.

When going to a new area, it's always wise to take along a friend or at the very least, tell someone where you are going and when you expect to return. Have fun and be safe on all your adventures.

All photos and text unless otherwise noted are courtesy of the author.

Other Schiffer Books by T. M. Gray:
Ghosts of Maine 978-0-7643-3113-8 $14.99
New England Graveside Tales 978-0-7643-3447-4 $19.99

Library of Congress Control Number: 2010928877

Designed by Mark David Bowyer
Type set in CosmicTwo / New Baskerville BT

ISBN: 978-0-7643-3585-3
Printed in China

Schiffer Books are available at special discounts for bulk purchases for sales promotions or premiums. Special editions, including personalized covers, corporate imprints, and excerpts can be created in large quantities for special needs. For more information contact the publisher:

Published by Schiffer Publishing Ltd.
4880 Lower Valley Road
Atglen, PA 19310
Phone: (610) 593-1777; Fax: (610) 593-2002
E-mail: Info@schifferbooks.com

For the largest selection of fine reference books on this and related subjects, please visit our web site at
www.schifferbooks.com
We are always looking for people to write books on new and related subjects.
If you have an idea for a book
please contact us at the above address.

This book may be purchased from the publisher.
Include $5.00 for shipping.
Please try your bookstore first.
You may write for a free catalog.

In Europe, Schiffer books are distributed by
Bushwood Books
6 Marksbury Ave.
Kew Gardens
Surrey TW9 4JF England
Phone: 44 (0) 20 8392-8585; Fax: 44 (0) 20 8392-9876
E-mail: info@bushwoodbooks.co.uk
Website: www.bushwoodbooks.co.uk

CONTENTS

Introduction

In the first volume of *New England Graveside Tales*, we delved into many of the mysteries concerning the natural environment. Volume II is a bit darker as much of it involves *human* nature. We'll break new ground with the long-standing ghost stories of America's earliest documented poltergeist and a couple of our oldest hauntings, and investigate the facts concerning the unsolved murders of the Borden family. You'll also find interesting places open to the public: castles and towers, eclectic museums, strange houses, and the locations of some of New England's most famous gravesites.

From there, look to the night skies and explore four of the most famous and chilling UFO abduction cases that happened right here in New England. Then head back to earth, about six feet deep, and learn the truth about vampires.

New England was the birthplace of the American vampire. Forget the Hollywood version with the satin cape and pretty porcelain fangs; these vampires don't sparkle. No one in their right mind would want to join their ranks, even if it meant living forever. These creatures, born of utter desperation, eventually gave rise to the myths we know today.

Lastly, take a long, hard look at one of the darkest eras in American history: when no man, woman, child, or beast was safe from the tyranny of the law…and the number accused listed in this book fall short of the hundreds who were persecuted for witchcraft. Many of their so-called "crimes" seem far-fetched, even fanciful by today's standards, but back then, even the most outrageous accusations were taken seriously, often with deadly outcomes. Salem, Massachusetts, remains America's witch capital…a vivid reminder of why we must be ever vigilant against intolerance and injustice. True, there is a carnival-esque atmosphere to some attractions in the old city, but one only has to look deeper to find the real scares. I've listed some of the more serious places to visit, for those interested in facing the darker side of colonial history.

Can you come back into the light unscathed and untouched by these encounters in the dark? I hope not, for as George Santayana once warned:

> "Those who do not remember the past are condemned to repeat it."

T. M. Gray
Birch Harbor, Maine

New England
CANADA
Maine
Fort Kent
Vanburen
Caribou
Presque Isle
Mars Hill
Houlton
Millinocket
Macwahoc
Vanceboro
Jackman
Lee
Lincoln
Greenville
Dover-Foxcroft
Eastport
E. Machias
Machias
Dexter
Orono
Newport
Solon
Pittsfield
Hampden
Bangor
Brewer
Hancock
Ellsworth
Rangeley
Skowhegan
Norridgewock
Bucksport
Rumford
Waterville
Belfast
Bar Harbor
Vassalboro
AUGUSTA
Gardiner
Rockland
Deer Isle
Auburn
Lewiston
Brunswick
Westbrook
Portland
Saco
Scarborough
Biddeford
Vermont
New Hampshire
Newport
St. Albens
Hardwick
Winooski
Berlin
St. Johnsbury
Lancaster
Burlington
MONTPELIER
Littleton
Barre
Conway
Middlebury
Hanover
Lebanon
Laconia
Franklin
Rutland
Windsor
Newport
Rochester
York
Springfield
CONCORD
Dover
Kittery
Exeter
Portsmouth
Bellows Falls
Hampton
Keene
Manchester
Haverhill
Bennington
Nashua
Lawrence
Gloucester
Brattleboro
Lowell
Salem
Lynn
Saugus
N. Adams
Greenfield
Massachusetts
Cambridge
BOSTON
Pittsfield
Worcester
Quincy
Provincetown
Newton
Holyoke
Brockton
Westfield
Springfield
Taunton
Putnam
Manville
Freetown
Greenville
Connecticut
Fall River
PROVIDENCE
Hyannis
Mansfield
Torrington
HARTFORD
Warwick
New Bedford
Willimantic
Kingston
Waterbury
Norwich
Newport
Narragansett
Groton
Charlestown
Orange
New Haven
Mystic
Stonington
Georgetown
New London
Rhode Island
Milford
Norwalk
Stamford
Greenwich
New York

New England

Historic Hauntings

LITHOBOLIA

The story of Lithobolia, the rock-throwing devil, is the earliest known documentation of poltergeist-like activity recorded in North America. The story goes back to an eyewitness account written in 1682 by Secretary of the Colony, Richard Chamberlain, Esq. It took place in Great Island (now Newcastle), New Hampshire. Purportedly, George Walton laid claim to a piece of land, which an old woman believed belonged to her. She, supposedly a witch, cursed him, saying that he would never peacefully enjoy that piece of land.

Thereafter, one night in June, a shower of stones rained upon the Walton house. Everyone woke up and went outside. The air was still and quiet. Strangely, their front gate had been removed and taken some distance from the house. While they were outside, the rain of stones began again, driving the family back into the house.

They had to lock themselves in an inner room of the house to escape the battery of these flying missiles as they crashed in through the windows and down the chimney. This rain of stones and other items continued for four hours. Richard Chamberlain, who had been staying with the Walton family, was nearly struck in the head by a flying sledgehammer. One of the stones that slammed upon his bedroom door weighed 8½ pounds. Richard left it locked in his room and later found this same stone in another room.

Some of the stones were hot. Some which had been gathered took to the air soon after. The lead crossbars of the door casings were bent outward, proof that the force hurling the stones had come from within the house. George's daughters had been frightened by the sight of a hand thrust from the window of an unoccupied room.

These stones would dance to music. Cheese was crumbled upon the floor. An iron was found driven into a wall with a kettle hanging upon it. Small rocks and stones were pelted at George Walton as he worked in the fields. Bundles of hay were found in treetops, and small twists of hay were stuck about the kitchen.

Although no one was gravely injured, a half a brick was thrown into the cradle from which an infant had just been removed. One night, a series of several weapons flew into the kitchen and lit gently upon a family member while others fell lightly to the floor.

Pewter dishes were often tossed around the kitchen. Sometimes they were bent in the process. Books flew about. Shards from a window broken by stones were found in perfectly square pieces. As people watched, the stones cut down stalks of corn. Sometimes the sounds of snorting and whistling could be heard as the stones flew about.

Someone in the house came up with an idea to put an end to the madness: they put some urine in a cooking pot, along with some crooked pins, and began to boil the strange concoction. As the brew began to heat, stones flew up: one broke the cover of the pot, another broke the handle and spilled the contents. The pot was refilled and reheated, but another stone flew into it and broke the pot. Friends and neighbors of the Walton family, including merchants, a reverend, the Governor of West Jersey, and the Deputy Governor of Rhode Island, witnessed these events.

In September, while George Walton was on his way to Portsmouth for a hearing on this matter, he was struck in the head with a stone the size of a fist. Richard Chamberlain showed the stone to the President of the Council.

George Walton died soon after, presumably from the blow to his skull, and the stone-throwing devil, Lithobolia, ceased its mischief. Assuming the account is true: Was it the work of a poltergeist or an entity from another dimension? Or is that what poltergeist are – beings invisible to our eyes that come from another world or plane of existence? Or was this the result of a strange mass psychosis?

Nelly (Hooper) Butler

The Nelly (Hooper) Butler haunting is one of America's first documented, authentic ghost stories. Nelly was born about 1775, one of seven children of David and Joanna (Williams) Hooper. She married George Goodwin Butler. (In my book, *Ghosts of Maine*, I incorrectly assumed from early accounts that Machias was the setting of this haunting, but thanks to the exhaustive research of author Marcus LiBrizzi (*Dark Woods, Chill Waters*), the true location is actually Sullivan, Maine.)

An eyewitness to Nelly's haunting had his account published in a pamphlet titled *Immortality Proved by the Testimony of Sense* (1826). A fly leaf reads: "Immortality proved by phenomena that were witnessed by hundreds in the town of Sullivan, Maine, in the year 1800. Published by an eyewitness, the Reverend Abraham Cummings, a man eminent in learning and piety; a graduate of Harvard University."

The story goes like this: After ten months of marriage, Nelly died in childbirth, along with her baby. After her death, the widowed George Butler fell in love with Lydia Blaisdell, born in 1787, the sixth of seven children born to Captain Abner and Mrs. (Card) Blaisdell. Captain Blaisdell along with Moses Butler (George's father), vehemently opposed the match. The reasons for their opposition are not given. Perhaps Moses Butler thought it was too soon after Nelly's death for his son to take up with another woman. There were some mysterious circumstances concerning Nelly's death (foul play was more than implied – there was a court trial), and certain allegations may have upset Lydia's father.

At any rate, Nelly's ghost appeared to the families involved (including her own), seemingly in an attempt to appease them to accept the romance of Captain Butler and Lydia Blaisdell. In these manifestations, her ghost spoke and was able to convince everyone that this was no mere parlor trick; she attested that Heaven itself destined the Butler-Blaisdell union.

According to the story, shortly before Nelly died, her husband promised never to remarry if something were to happen to her. After her death, however, George found himself unable to keep that promise. Strange noises started occurring in the Blaisdell home; the loudest was noted on August 9, 1799. Then on January 2, 1800, a female voice in the cellar of the Blaisdell home identified herself as Nelly (Hooper) Butler and requested the presence of her father, David Hooper, her husband, George Butler, as well as Lydia's father, Captain Blaisdell. All three met there and were convinced this was indeed Nelly's ghost.

Man and his Ghost Bride. *Photo by William Hope*, c1905. (Most of William Hope's ghost photos have been debunked as tricks of photography.)

In May 1800, Nelly's ghost materialized wearing "a shining white garment" before twenty people gathered in Captain Blaisdell's cellar. According to one eyewitness, "At first the apparition was a mere mass of light, then it grew into a personal form, about as tall as myself…the glow of the apparition had a constant, tremulous motion. At last the personal form became shapeless, expanded every way and then vanished in a moment." Some described her as having "a shining halo around her head." Her voice, according to some, was "shrill but mild and pleasant."

On another occasion, Nelly appeared before 200 people where she foretold the deaths of Captain Blaisdell's wife and his father, as well as the future marriage of Lydia Blaisdell to her widowed husband, George Butler. When Captain Blaisdell asked Nelly why she did not appear in the house (only in the cellar), she simply told him, "I do not wish to frighten the children."

At the time, Reverend Abraham Cummings did not believe in ghosts or hauntings. He became alarmed that people were taking Nelly so seriously, especially when it came to her sermons. He'd heard people repeating things she said, such as in an appearance in March 1806: "Although my body is consumed and all turned to dust, my soul is as much alive as before I left the body."

He went to the Butler home intent on exposing the ghost as a parlor trick, but something convinced him otherwise and that something was the ghost of Nelly (Hooper) Butler.

William Oliver Stevens describes their strange encounter in this book: *Unbidden Guests: A Book of Real Ghosts* (1945). According to Mr. Stevens, "white rocks floated up from the ground, joined together and took the shape of a rose-tinged orb, which suddenly flashed and manifested into the form of a child-sized woman." When Reverend Cummings spoke to it, "the figure expanded to normal size." She was described as "glorious with rays of light shining from her head all about and reaching to the ground."

Convinced of the ghost's authenticity, Reverend Abraham Cummings published *Immortality Proved by the Testimony of Science* shortly before his death on August 31, 1827, in North Yarmouth, Maine. It includes many of the forty depositions and affidavits given by eyewitnesses who saw and heard the ghost.

Lydia Blaisdell and George Butler married, but Lydia died shortly thereafter…in childbirth, just as Nelly had before her. After Lydia's death, Nelly's ghost did not vanish immediately, but continued in like manner for some time. Nelly's ghost, according to Reverend Cummings, requested the re-interment of her infant's remains, and the reburial in a different spot. With over eighty people present at the solemn re-interment, Nelly's ghost appeared, singing hymns, quoting scripture, and praying.

It was said that George Goodwin Butler, in great remorse, never married again, and died on April 26, 1826, at age 55, however, some genealogies show a third marriage on September 12, 1805, to Mary Googins who bore him seven children. Mary died in 1862 at age 81.

Lizzie Borden

Think of a female axe murderer and one name comes to mind: Lizzie Borden. The crime was so infamous, children still sing a chilling nursery rhyme about her: "Lizzie Borden took an axe and gave her mother forty whacks. When she saw what she had done, she gave her father forty-one." A newspaper reporter around the time of her trial created that rhyme; the number of "whacks" is exaggerated, and although a jury found her innocent of the crimes, the questions remain: Did Lizzie Borden get away with murder? And what ghosts haunt the Borden House?

To investigate the mystery, let's go back in time to Fall River, Massachusetts in 1892. The mode of transportation was by streetcar, horse, wagon, or train. Indoor plumbing was vogue. Women weren't allowed to vote. But for a handful of exceptions, they were quite limited in terms of professional career (for example, many were nurses, but few became doctors; many were schoolteachers, few became professors). Most ladies lived with their parents until they married; it was common for fathers, as well as husbands, to expect complete obedience from them. Many married very young and sometimes they died in childbirth. At the time, pregnancy was treated more like an illness than a natural condition.

On the other hand, most women of this era were usually treated with a high degree of chivalry. Ladies in the middle and upper classes tended to lead what we would call *sheltered* lives, and great care was taken to shield them from any vulgarity. Rarely was such a woman accused of committing a serious crime and if she had to go to court, she was judged by men and usually acquitted.

These social factors helped set the stage for the turmoil, upheaval, and eventual outcome of the murders at 92 Second Street, Fall River, Massachusetts, on August 4, 1892.

Up until that time, Elizabeth Andrew Borden aka "Lizzie," age 32, was an unmarried Sunday School teacher. Prim and proper, she and her older sister, Emma Lenora, lived at home with their father, Andrew Jackson Borden, and their stepmother, Abby Durfee (Gray) Borden. They had an Irish maid, Bridget Sullivan, who lived on the third story of their home, and while not considered upper crust, the Bordens certainly were *upper* middle class. Andrew Borden was noted for being careful with money. He had served as president of the Union Savings Bank as well as director of several corporations in town, and had accumulated stock in local businesses. He was not particularly liked among his peers; many thought him stingy, for despite his apparent wealth, the Borden home lacked gaslights and indoor plumbing.

That may have been one matter of contention between Andrew and his daughters. Another difficulty may have concerned certain changes he was planning for his will.

Lizzie Borden

The Borden House

Emma Borden

Bridget Sullivan

Andrew Borden

Abby Borden

John Morse

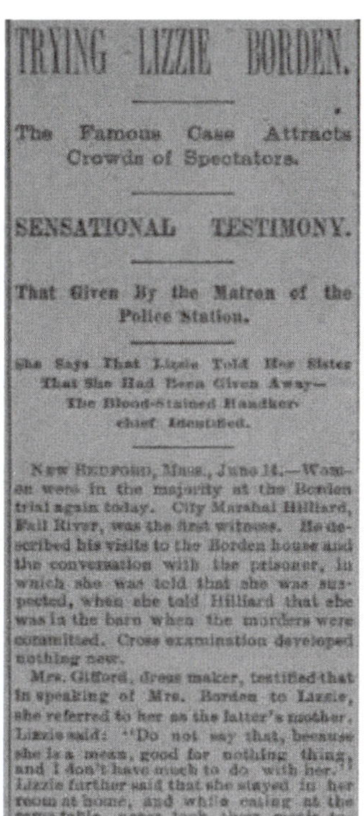

TRYING LIZZIE BORDEN.

The Famous Case Attracts Crowds of Spectators.

SENSATIONAL TESTIMONY.

That Given By the Matron of the Police Station.

She Says That Lizzie Told Her Sister That She Had Been Given Away—The Blood-Stained Handkerchief Identified.

NEW BEDFORD, Mass., June 14.—Women were in the majority at the Borden trial again today. City Marshal Hilliard, Fall River, was the first witness. He described his visits to the Borden house and the conversation with the prisoner, in which she was told that she was suspected, when she told Hilliard that she was in the barn when the murders were committed. Cross examination developed nothing new.

Mrs. Gifford, dress maker, testified that in speaking of Mrs. Borden to Lizzie, she referred to her as the latter's mother. Lizzie said: "Do not say that, because she is a mean, good for nothing thing, and I don't have much to do with her." Lizzie further said that she stayed in her room at home, and while eating at the same table, never took their meals together.

Hatchet found in cellar

Did she do it?

Evidence seemed to be stacked against her…

Whatever the problems of the Borden household, apparently everything came to a head on August 4, 1892.

That morning, Emma, the oldest Borden daughter, was fifteen miles away in Fairhaven visiting friends. The maid, Bridget Sullivan, along with Andrew, Abby, and Lizzie Borden had been sick to their stomachs the night before. Abby confided suspicions of intentional poisoning earlier that morning to Dr. Seabury Bowen, the Borden family's physician. She had no idea Lizzie tried to purchase hydrogen cyanide from Smith's Drugstore the day before. The pharmacist had refused to sell it to her, even though she claimed she needed it to remove insects from a sealskin cape. Thus, the doctor ignored Abby's suspicions and diagnosed the ailment as food poisoning. After seeing Abby, the doctor arrived at the Bordens' to check on Andrew, but Andrew was apparently in good health.

John Vinnicum Morse, uncle to the Borden sisters, had been staying with the Bordens at the time. John was the brother of Sarah Anthony (Morse) Borden (Andrew Borden's first wife). Sarah and Andrew had three girls together but Alice Esther Borden, the middle child, died before her second birthday. Sarah herself died five years later (1863) due to uterine congestion and spinal disease. Within two years of her death, Andrew Borden married Abby when Emma was age 14 and Lizzie was 5.

John Morse was not at the Borden home on that fateful August morning. Earlier that morning, Andrew Borden left the house around 9 a.m. to make his usual rounds downtown. Bridget Sullivan was outside washing the first-story windows of the home. Lizzie was in and out of the house; at one point, she had gone to the barn to look for fishing sinkers (she planned to use them on a fishing trip the next day). Abby was upstairs on the second floor, straightening up the guest room where John was staying.

Around 10:45 a.m., Andrew returned from his rounds and Bridget unlocked the door to let him inside. She then retired upstairs to her bed, still ill from the night before.

At 11:10 a.m., Lizzie shouted to Bridget: "Come quick, Maggie! (The Bordens had a former maid named Maggie.) Father's dead! Somebody's come in and killed him!"

Bridget rushed downstairs but Lizzie prevented her entry into the sitting room. She told the maid to hurry and fetch Dr. Bowen. Bridget ran across the road to the doctor's house, but his wife told her the doctor was out on a call. Bridget then ran back to the Borden house. Lizzie bade her to fetch their neighbor, Alice Russell. While Bridget was gone, another neighbor, Adelaide Churchill called out to Lizzie, asking if something was wrong. Lizzie asked her over, saying, "Someone has killed Father!"

Mrs. Churchill asked Lizzie where Abby was, and Lizzie replied that Abby received a note earlier and had gone to tend to a sick friend. Mrs. Churchill sent her handyman to summon help. The police were called at 11:15.

Before they arrived, Bridget returned along with Dr. Bowen, who went into the sitting room to find Andrew Borden gruesomely murdered on the mohair sofa. His skull was cleaved to pieces; there was blood everywhere. The doctor asked for a sheet to cover him up.

Meanwhile, Lizzie told the maid she was "positive" she heard Abby come in and sent her upstairs to find her. Because Bridget seemed quite shaken, Mrs. Churchill joined her. They found Abby Borden lying facedown in a pool of blood on the floor of the guest bedroom between the bed and dresser. Mrs. Churchill ran downstairs declaring, "There's another one!"

Upon examination, the doctor found that Abby had been struck from behind. The flesh on her head and neck was reduced to ribbons. He administered a tranquilizer to Lizzie, and sent for medical examiner Dr. William A. Dolan to assist with the autopsies.

Meanwhile, Officer George W. Allen of the Freetown Police Department arrived at the Borden house. He took one look at Andrew Borden's body and quickly left to fetch more officers. Seven policemen returned with him to the Borden house.

By chance, the medical examiner, Dr. Dolan, had yet to receive Dr. Bowen's telegram, but was on his way through town when he noticed the commotion going on at the Borden home. He stopped to find out what was happening. The time was now around 11:45 a.m.

At 4 p.m., autopsies of both Bordens were conducted on the dining room table of their home. Their sheet-covered bodies were left there overnight. (Bridget refused to sleep in the Borden house that night. When she returned the next day, it was to pack her things and leave permanently.)

The outcome of the autopsies showed that Abbey was probably killed first, having been struck once between the upper shoulder blades, and eighteen times in the back of her head. Andrew had been struck eleven times from his nose to his left ear.

The police searched for the murder weapon(s), and in a box of coal dust in the cellar, they discovered a hatchet with a broken handle. While they conducted their investigation, people were coming and going in and out of the Borden house.

A few days later, Dr. Dolan interrupted the Borden's burial at the Oak Grove Cemetery, and performed a second autopsy in a receiving vault on the cemetery grounds, removing the heads of the murder victims as evidence. (When the murder trial was over, the skulls would be re-interred.)

Before it was over, police had a list of forty-two suspects.

Every one of the leads turned out to be a dead-end, except four: John Morse, Bridget Sullivan, and the two Borden sisters. Emma and John were able to provide alibis. Bridget never changed one iota of her statements; however, Lizzie's story changed several times throughout questioning.

Just eight days later, neighbor Alice Russell recalled having seen Lizzie burning a dress in the kitchen stove just two days after the murders. Police arrested Lizzie on August 11th.

Lizzie then used her inheritance to hire a team of competent lawyers, who declared their client's innocence and tried to prove the murderer was an angry hired hand whom Andrew had refused to pay. Several witnesses testified that they had seen several strange men in the area around the time of the murders.

The judge was clearly biased in Lizzie's favor and the jury followed suit. On June 20, 1893, after a one-hour deliberation, Elizabeth Andrew Borden was found not guilty by reasonable doubt.

A free woman, Lizzie moved out of her parents' house and bought a stylish home, at 306 French Street. Nevertheless, for the most part, she was shunned by upper-class society. Once a Sunday School teacher, now she was unable to attend church. Emma moved in with her; she wasn't ostracized like her sister and became a devoted churchgoer.

Lizzie named her new home "Maplecroft," and took on a new name for herself as well: Lisbeth. In 1987, she was charged with shoplifting, but settled out of court. Then she met actress Nance O'Neill.

Lisbeth threw a lavish party for her new actress friend. Emma moved out of Maplecroft and eventually moved to Newmarket, New Hampshire. Lisbeth's infatuation (whether platonic or romantic) with the actress lasted about two years.

On June 1, 1927, Lisbeth died from complications after gall bladder surgery, and strangely, Emma died nine days later when she fell down the stairs of her New Hampshire home. Lisbeth left her estate to charitable organizations for animals; Emma left hers to humanitarian projects. Both sisters were buried beside their parents and their 2-year-old sister at Oak Grove Cemetery.

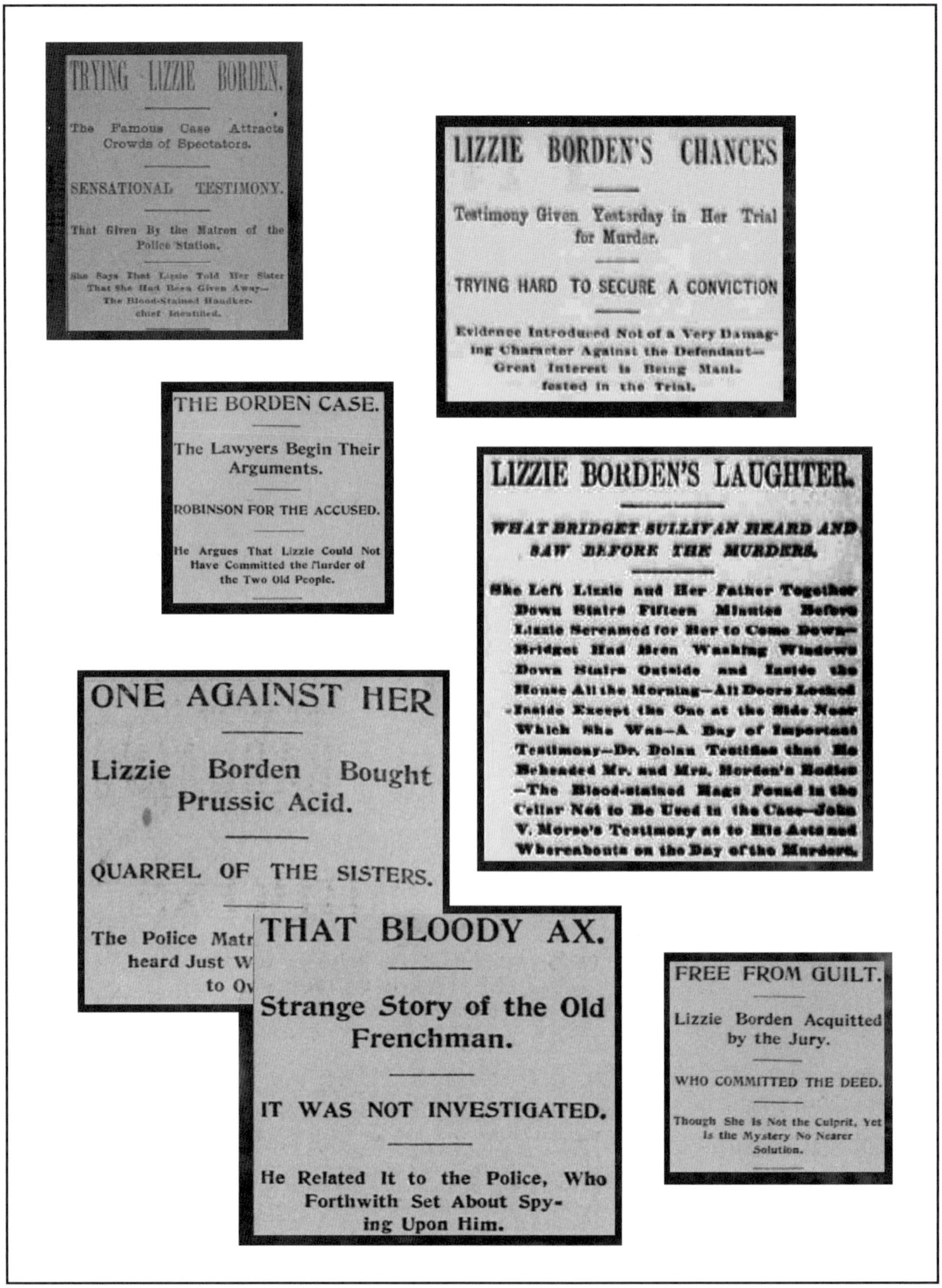

TRYING LIZZIE BORDEN.

The Famous Case Attracts Crowds of Spectators.

SENSATIONAL TESTIMONY.

That Given By the Matron of the Police Station.

She Says That Lizzie Told Her Sister That She Had Been Given Away—The Blood-Stained Handkerchief Identified.

LIZZIE BORDEN'S CHANCES

Testimony Given Yesterday in Her Trial for Murder.

TRYING HARD TO SECURE A CONVICTION

Evidence Introduced Not of a Very Damaging Character Against the Defendant—Great Interest is Being Manifested in the Trial.

THE BORDEN CASE.

The Lawyers Begin Their Arguments.

ROBINSON FOR THE ACCUSED.

He Argues That Lizzie Could Not Have Committed the Murder of the Two Old People.

LIZZIE BORDEN'S LAUGHTER.

WHAT BRIDGET SULLIVAN HEARD AND SAW BEFORE THE MURDERS.

She Left Lizzie and Her Father Together Down Stairs Fifteen Minutes Before Lizzie Screamed for Her to Come Down—Bridget Had Been Washing Windows Down Stairs Outside and Inside the House All the Morning—All Doors Locked Inside Except the One at the Side Near Which She Was—A Day of Important Testimony—Dr. Dolan Testifies that He Beheaded Mr. and Mrs. Borden's Bodies—The Blood-stained Rags Found in the Cellar Not to Be Used in the Case—John V. Morse's Testimony as to His Acts and Whereabouts on the Day of the Murders.

ONE AGAINST HER

Lizzie Borden Bought Prussic Acid.

QUARREL OF THE SISTERS.

The Police Matr... heard Just W... to Ov...

THAT BLOODY AX.

Strange Story of the Old Frenchman.

IT WAS NOT INVESTIGATED.

He Related It to the Police, Who Forthwith Set About Spying Upon Him.

FREE FROM GUILT.

Lizzie Borden Acquitted by the Jury.

WHO COMMITTED THE DEED.

Though She Is Not the Culprit, Yet is the Mystery No Nearer Solution.

Newspaper Headline Clippings about Lizzie Borden's Trial.

However, the question lingers to this day: Did Lizzie really kill her father and stepmother?

In 2004, Thomas P. Mauriello, Professor of Criminalistics at the University of Maryland, and Tom Lange, retired LAPD Homicide Detective, conducted a forensic investigation at the Borden house, which is now a popular bed and breakfast. They conducted tests and sprayed Luminol for traces of blood. The amazing results were shown on The Discovery Channel's "Lizzie Borden Had an Axe" in 2004.

Unfortunately, we will never truly know who murdered the Bordens or the reason why. All that is left are speculations and ghosts. And speaking of ghosts, the Travel Channel's show, *Scariest Places on Earth,* has named the Lizzie Borden house the #1 scariest place on earth. People have seen ghosts in the Borden house, and some have been physically touched by them.

It is said sometimes murder runs in the family, and history repeats itself. If Lizzie did indeed kill her father and stepmother…perhaps, she was following a pattern of crime that went back 200 years.

On the early evening of February 8, 1673, 73-year-old Rebecca (Briggs) Cornell of Portsmouth, Rhode Island, died under mysterious circumstances. Her burned body was found in front of her fireplace. At the time of her death, her son, Thomas, and his family were eating dinner in an adjacent room. Less than two weeks later, 42-year-old Thomas was arrested for Rebecca's murder.

The court ordered Rebecca's body exhumed because her brother, John Briggs, awoke on the night of February 12th to find her ghost standing in his bedroom. "See how I was burnt with fire," the apparition repeated to him in a pleading tone. This convinced John to press for an autopsy on his sister's body. A chest wound revealed the probable cause of death.

Thomas was found guilty of her murder and sentenced to death by hanging. He was the 5th great grandfather of Lizzie Andrew Borden.

Visitors can tour the Lizzie Borden house (bed and breakfast), and they are welcome to book a room for the night, *if they dare*. The Borden Collection at the Fall River Historical Society Museum contains many artifacts related to the trial, including the hatchet found in the cellar.

Lizzie Borden Bed and Breakfast

230 Second Street,
Fall River, MA 02720
Phone: (508) 675-7333
Web: www.lizzie-borden.com

Tours daily on the hour 11 a.m. - 3 p.m. Admission charged. (Call to verify)

The Fall River Historical Society

451 Rock Street
Fall River, MA 02720
Phone: (508) 679-1071
Web: www.lizzieborden.org

Open May - October, Tuesday - Friday, 9 a.m. - 4 p.m. Tours every hour from 9 a.m. to 3 p.m. except noon. June - September, Saturday and Sunday, 1 p.m. - 4:30 p.m. Weekend tours from 1 p.m. to 4 p.m. on the hour.

Admission as of 2009: $6.00 Adults, $4 Children, ages 6-14. Call for Group Rates.

The Shrieking Woman of Marblehead

On September 21, 1690, a Spanish ship was captured and brought to Marblehead Harbor by cutthroat Captain Ned Low and his pirate crew. They had murdered everyone on board with exception of a beautiful English lady.

At night, they brought her ashore at Lovis Cove and there they raped her and stole her rings by cutting off her fingers before murdering her. The women and children living nearby heard the victim's bloodcurdling screams, but none were able to help her. Their men were out on their fishing vessels at the Grand Banks, and the families left behind feared for themselves being at the mercy of the pirates.

Her pitiful screams pierced the night: "Lord, save me! Mercy! Oh Lord Jesus, save me!" This was so terrible to hear; mothers clamped their hands over their children's ears, wept and prayed for the poor creature on the beach. Then the night grew eerily quiet.

Her body was buried the next day above the waterline of the beach, but on the anniversary of that dreadful crime, her spirit refuses to rest. For hundreds of years, locals and visitors alike have heard her screams. The beach at Lovis Cove was named 'Screaming Woman Beach.'

In the mid-1980s, one of my readers wrote to tell me about his encounter near Fort Sewall. While walking toward the fort, he saw a woman screaming near the flagpole. His entire body froze and he wasn't able to move until she began to fade away – that's when he realized he'd seen the ghost of the screaming woman.

Shocked, he turned around and walked straight past his car. His wife got out of the car and caught up with him, asking him what was wrong, but he was shocked beyond words. Then he managed to mumble and pointed to the fort. It took a few moments for him to recover and tell her what he saw. The next day he contacted someone who worked at the fort and reported the encounter.

At least one paranormal investigator has been able to record EVPs in the area. One is a voice yelling for help. Photographs taken near the beach sometimes show strange lights.

Fort Sewall is open year round, everyday from sunrise to sunset. Parking is limited.

Fort Sewall

Front Street, Route 114
Marblehead, MA 01945

The Screeching Woman of Marblehead by Howard Pyle, 1892.

Places to Visit

Mystery Hill: America's Stonehenge

P. O. Box 84 (mailing address)
105 Haverhill Road (physical address)
Salem, New Hampshire 03079
Phone: (603) 893-8300
Email: info@stonehengeusa.com
Web: www.stonehengeusa.com

Open year round from 9 a.m. to 5 p.m. Closed Thanksgiving Day and Christmas. Admission as of 2009: Adults $9.50, Seniors $8.50, Children ages 6-12 $6.50, Children under 5, free. Groups welcome. No pets, please.

One of the most ancient man-made sites in the United States can be found in Salem, New Hampshire: America's Stonehenge is an outdoor museum that takes about an hour to tour (self-guided).

No one knows who constructed the maze-like passages, estimated to be over 4,000 years old. This does not look like the Stonehenge in England, but its builders were certainly familiar with astronomy and probably used it to determine lunar and solar events. Some of the inscriptions found at the site were determined to be of Phoenician and Iberian origin. The site also served as an important resting place in the Underground Railroad.

Inside the stone calendar, visitors can examine the 4.5-ton granite sacrificial table. There are numerous stone chambers to explore, and visitors are encouraged to come up with their own answers as to who built them and what purposes they might have served. Stone tablets found on the site are believed to have something to do with the worship of Bel/Baal. The tablets can be seen at America's Stonehenge Visitor's Center.

Barnum Museum

820 Main Street
Bridgeport, Connecticut 06604-4912
Phone: (203) 331-1104
Web: www.barnum-museum.org

The Barnum Museum is open 10 a.m. to 4:30 p.m. Tuesday through Saturday, and from 12 noon - 4:30 p.m. on Sundays. (Last admission is at 3:45 p.m.) Closed Mondays and holidays.

Admission as of 2009: Adults $7, Seniors and Students $5, Children 4-17 $4. Children 3 and younger, Free. The museum is handicap accessible.

P. T. (Phineas Taylor) Barnum, a native son of Bethel, Connecticut, was one of the country's most famous showmen, and his museum in Bridgeport has been open since 1893. Interesting items in the collection include the famous Feejee mermaid, a piece of General Tom Thumb's 1893 wedding cake, the stuffed elephant Baby Bridgeport, a 1,000-foot model of a five-ring circus, memorabilia from the Industrial Age, and an Egyptian mummy.

The mummy, Pa-Ib, a mysterious 4,000-year-old Egyptian female, was given to the museum by P.T. Barnum's wife, Nancy, in 1892 and was recently authenticated by researchers using high-tech scanning equipment.

The original museum building, owned by the City of Bridgeport, is listed in the National Register of Historic Places and was designed by the architectural firm Longstaff and Hurd. The museum was originally named The Barnum Institute of Science and History.

The Barnum Museum. *Photographed by Kay Page Greaser, 2008, and provided by The Barnum Museum.*

Hope Cemetery

175 Maple Avenue,
Barre, Vermont 05641

Hope Cemetery is open everyday during daylight hours. A small fee is charged for a guided tour, but most people drive or walk through the cemetery on their own.

Hope Cemetery, the Rock of Ages Granite Quarry and the Whispering Statue are all in Barre, Vermont, a city known the "Granite Capitol of the World."

Hope Cemetery was established in 1895 and contains over 10,000 headstones and monuments, all fashioned from "Barre Grey" granite. Many are truly amazing works of art. It takes the better part of an hour to drive through the 65-acre burial ground.

Rock of Ages Granite Quarry

558 Graniteville Road
Barre, Vermont 05641
Phone: (802) 476-3119

Open May - October, Monday - Saturday 8:30 a.m. - 5 p.m. Sundays 10 a.m. - 5 p.m.

The Rock of Ages Quarry offers free tours from June to October. It is the source of most of the country's granite headstones and all of Barre, Vermont's remarkable monuments. The quarry museum offers a video showing how granite is quarried, and the shuttle tour takes visitors into the granite pits. They even have a granite bowling alley. Small granite samples are free.

Whispering Statue

Main Street
Barre, Vermont 05641

The Whispering Statue is a war memorial in City Hall Park in the town center of Barre, Vermont. Built in the 1920s, it depicts a young soldier with a robe and shield. Its official name is *Youth Triumphant*. The wall behind it is the real "whisperer," but to get the statue to "whisper," take a seat on one end of the semi-circular granite bench surrounding the statue, and have a friend sit on the other end. The statue should be between you both. Now have your friend say something in a normal, speaking voice. Because of bouncing acoustics off the granite statue and wall, it will sound like your friend is sitting right next to you or standing behind you.

Belcourt Castle

657 Bellevue Avenue
Newport, Rhode Island 02840
Phone: (401) 846-0669
Web: www.belcourtcastle.org

Open Monday - Saturday 10 a.m. - 4 p.m., Sundays 12 noon - 5 p.m. Guided tours given hourly. Ghost tours usually take place at 5 p.m. on Thursdays and Saturdays, but check the website for the schedule.

Tour admission as of 2009: Adults $15, Seniors (age 65) $10 and College Students (with IDs) $10, Children ages 13-17 $7, Children ages 6-17 $5, Children under 5 Free.

Belcourt Castle was completed in 1894 as a summer estate for U.S. Representative Oliver Hazard Perry Belmont of New York. With 60 rooms spanning 50,000 square feet, it was designed by Richard Morris Hunt with many décor styles, most prominently Gothic and French Renaissance. It is Newport, Rhode Island's third largest mansion, and is operated by the Royal Arts Foundation.

Visitors can tour over a dozen rooms in the castle. Two chairs in the French Gothic Ballroom are said to contain spirits. The temperature surrounding one of the chairs is unusually cold compared to the rest of the room. The other chair has been known to eject hapless sitters. A suit of armor in the ballroom is reputedly haunted as well. (The man wearing it was struck in the eye by a spear, which went through his skull and emerged from the other side of his helmet.)

As of 2009, it is the only mansion in Newport owned privately and open to the public.

Belcourt Castle by Frank H. Child. *Courtesy Architectural Record,* 1895.

Woodman Institute Museum

P. O. Box 46 (mail address)
182 Central Avenue (physical address)
Dover, New Hampshire 03820
Phone: (603) 72-1038
Web: www.woodmaninstitutemuseum.com

Open Wednesday - Sunday 12:30 p.m. - 4:30 p.m. Open weekends only December - January. Closed February 1 - March 31. Closed holidays.

Admission: Adults $5, Students and Seniors $4, Children ages 14-16 $2, Children under 13 Free.

The Woodman Institute Museum in Dover, New Hampshire, has been in operation since 1916 and was funded by philanthropist Annie Woodman to encourage her city's education in history, science, and the arts. It is often called "a museum within a museum," for it encompasses three buildings and contains well over 800 relics of colonial and natural history. There is so much to see here, from preserved reptiles and insects, and taxidermied mammals to rare war memorabilia, and the biggest mineral collection north of Boston. The museum offers some real oddities such as a four-legged chicken and the Hall of Dolls.

Hammond Castle Museum

80 Hesperus Avenue,
Gloucester, Massachusetts 01930
Phone: (978) 283-2080
Web: www.hammondcastle.org

Hammond Castle Museum is open Tuesday - Sunday 10 a.m. - 4 p.m. (Last ticket sold at 3:30 p.m.)

Admission as of 2009: Adults $10, Seniors $8, Children ages 6-12 $6. Cash, Visa, Mastercard accepted. No American Express.

Call two weeks in advance to reserve a guided tour for tour bus and school groups. Personal cameras are welcome, but no tripods or commercial photography permitted. Not handicapped accessible.

Hammond Castle was completed in 1929 as a home for inventor Dr. John Hays Hammond, Jr., "the Father of Remote Control." The castle also housed the Hammond Research Corporation. It has been on the U.S. National Register of Historic Places since 1973.

Aside from being an avid collector of antiques and various curiosities, many of which can be seen at the castle, Dr. Hammond had an eccentric streak. Sometimes he would walk the grounds of his castle wearing a long monk's robe. He wrote many horror stories, but unfortunately, his father discouraged him from publishing. Dr. Hammond held séances in the castle and conducted scientific experiments to measure and enhance psychic energy. Some of these experiments included the use of a Faraday cage.

His circular library, containing a large collection of occult books, is said to be haunted. Custodians have found books lying open on his desk that were previously resting on the shelves. It was thought that some of the artifacts collected by Dr. Hammond actually brought spirits into his castle, while others assumed the Spiritualism experiments he, his wife, and their psychic friends conducted invited the continued presence of ghosts.

Over the years, numerous people have reported seeing ghosts at the castle, as well as hearing disembodied voices.

Dr. Hammond died February 12, 1965. He and his wife, Irene, were buried in a nearby mausoleum with steps going down directly into the ocean. Their dozens of Siamese cats, preserved in formaldehyde, were buried with them. Sometimes guests report hearing cats meowing near the sepulcher.

In 2008, the Hammonds' remains were reinterred in the Castle's Cat Garden in preparation for the sale of the mausoleum property.

Visitors to the castle are welcome to take a self-guided tour and explore through two towers of rooms, a secret passageway, and the courtyard. Annual events include a Psychic Fair (usually held in July), Candlelit Tours in July and August, and Castle of the Damned for Halloween, which is organized by a theatrical group and differs from most Halloween haunted houses because the actors don't try to startle you into a cheap shot scare. Instead, they really frighten visitors by all the work they put into the scenery. **Not** recommended for young children. (Visit www.pastimesentertainment.com/castle.html for more info and this year's schedule. Proceeds benefit restoration projects at Hammond Castle.)

Old State House Museum

800 Main Street
Hartford, Connecticut 06103
Phone: (860) 522-6766
Web: www.ctoldstatehouse.cga.ct.gov/

The John Steward Museum of Curiosities is open during Old State House hours: Tuesday - Saturday, 10 a.m. - 5 p.m. in the summer; Monday - Friday, 9 a.m. - 5 p.m. the rest of the year. Closed Sundays and holidays.

Admission as of 2009: Adults $6, Children $3, Children under age 5 Free, Students with ID $3, Seniors $3, AAA Members (with card) $3, Active and Veteran Military members (with card) Free. Parking available at West Constitution Plaza Garage, $5.

Built in 1796, Hartford, Connecticut's Old State House Museum has been a National Historic Landmark since 1960. The Connecticut Office of Legislative Management has run Hartford, Connecticut's Old State House Museum since 2008. While the first two floors of the museum are devoted to Hartford's history and legislative past, The John Steward Museum of Curiosities is located on the third floor. It was part of the Old State House in 1797, and is one of the country's oldest museums.

John Steward was a famous portrait painter who began collecting fascinating and strange items in his studio at the State House. His collection became the Museum of Natural and Other Curiosities.

Included in the collection are a two-headed calf, a two-headed pig fetus, stuffed albino mammals, an 8-foot long alligator, birds, shellfish (an oyster shell weighing 234 pounds) and butterflies, along with some weird mechanical devices. Most items in the collection are recreations of the originals. (In 1808, the museum ran out of space and had to relocate, and many of its items were lost over the years.)

Old State House, Hartford, Connecticut.

The Paper House

52 Pigeon Hill Street
Rockport, Massachusetts 01966
Phone: (978) 546-2629
Web: http://www.paperhouserockport.com/

Open daily April - October. Hours: 10 a.m. - 5 p.m. (Call to verify)
Admission as of 2009: Adults $1.50, Children ages 6-14 $1

The Paper House in Rockport, Massachusetts was constructed almost completely from newspaper. Even the furniture inside is made of paper.

Elis F. Stenman, a mechanical engineer, built the two-story home. He may have gotten his inspiration for the house after designing machines that make paper chips. What turned into a hobby eventually became his summer cottage. Beginning in 1922, the Stenman family rolled, pasted and varnished around 100,000 newspapers.

Almost everything inside is made from rolled paper. The major exceptions are the wooden frame, floors and roof of the house, the electrical wiring, plumbing, and a working fireplace made of brick.

The Dog Chapel

143 Parks Road
St. Johnsbury, Vermont 05819
Phone: (802) 748-2700
Web: www.dogmt.com

Open June - October (November - May by appointment only) Monday - Saturday 10 a.m. - 5 p.m. Sunday 11 a.m. - 4 p.m.
Admission Free.

Near Death Experiences (NDEs) often affect people in profound ways. Author, artist, and woodcarver, Stephen Huneck, had an NDE in 1997 when he was suffering acute respiratory distress syndrome after falling down a flight of stairs. Acute Respiratory Distress Syndrome is the most serious lung injury there is with a mortality rate of between thirty to forty percent. Stephen remained in a coma for two long months, then one night he died for about five minutes. During his NDE, Stephen had a spiritual encounter with a gentle canine spirit. This inspired him to build The Dog Chapel on Dog Mountain.

The Dog Chapel was built after Stephen recovered from his illness, which included learning to walk again. He has described the chapel as the largest artwork of his life, as well as the most personal.

Dog Mountain is a must-stop for dogs and the people who love them; its 400 acres are devoted to man's best friend. Dogs are encouraged to get out of the car to walk, run, and play here. The Dog Chapel is nondenominational and, of course, dogs are always welcome. The four walls are remembrance walls covered with thousands of notes and photos of visitors' beloved, dearly-departed canines. Stephen's woodcarvings of pets decorate the chapel, and a dog's favorite things: playing with a ball, eating ice cream cones and being patted are depicted in the stained glass windows. There's even a doggie-door so dogs can come and go as they please. There are no sermons, but soft music plays in the background.

The Dog Chapel does not charge admission or ask for donations, and no, dogs are not married there. It's just a nice place to go to remember the dogs who touched your life, and Dog Mountain is a real treat for your canine companion.

THE TITANIC MUSEUM

P. O. Box 51053
208 Main Street (physical address)
Indian Orchard, Massachusetts 01151-0053
Phone: (413) 543-4770 (Call only during EST business hours.)
Web: www.titanic1.org/museum
www.titanichistoricalsociety.org

Open Daily year round, Monday - Friday 10 a.m. - 4 p.m., Saturday 10 a.m. - 3 p.m. Closed Sundays and holidays. Self-guided. Children must be accompanied by an adult. Average visit lasts about an hour.

Admission as of 2009: Adults: $4, Children under 12 $2, Children under 6 Free.

The Great Titanic Disaster. *Courtesy George Grantham Bain Collection, Library of Congress, 1912.*

The Titanic Museum in Indian Orchard, Massachusetts, was the first of its kind to honor the ship and those who took her maiden voyage. It was started in 1963 by the Titanic Historical Society, the world's largest Titanic organization. Society president, Ed Kamuda, founded the Titanic Historical Society when one of the Titanic survivors died and his belongings where thrown into the city dump. He knew he had to do something to preserve the Titanic-related items.

Many of the Society's collection of rare Titanic survivor artifacts can be seen at The Titanic Museum. Survivors and their families donated much of it. Nothing in the museum was taken from the sunken ship.

Of course, no artifacts exist from the *Titanic* concerning the forbidden romance of Jack Dawson and Rose DeWitt Bukater, two fictional characters from the 1997 blockbuster film, *Titanic*. In The Titanic Museum, however, is a rare commemorative sculpture of Rose's famous couch pose. (In real life, there was a *Joseph* Dawson who is sometimes confused with the fictional Jack. Joseph was a coal trimmer who went down with the ship, as did eighty percent of his crewmates.)

The museum contains interesting artifacts such as Mrs. Astor's lifejacket, flotsam recovered after the sinking, the launching menus and much more.

Edward Gorey House

8 Strawberry Lane
Yarmouthport, Massachusetts 02675
Phone: (508) 362-3909
Web: www.edwardgoreyhouse.org/

Open around mid-April to late December, every weekend and on some Wednesdays, Thursdays and Fridays. Hours: 11 a.m. - 4 p.m. Sunday hours: 12 noon - 4 p.m. (Call or check website to verify schedule.)

Admission as of 2009: Adults $5, Seniors and Students $3, Children ages 6-12 $2, Children under age 6 Free.

Author-illustrator extraordinaire Edward St. John Gorey (1925-2000) lived in this Cape Cod home after he left New York City in 1960. Although called "The Edward Gorey House," it is also known as "Elephant House," and it celebrates his life and work. He is probably best remembered for his somewhat macabre (and wonderful) illustrations, but he also wrote plays, and in 1978, he won a Tony Award for Best Costume Design for Broadway's *Dracula*.

On self-guided and docent-guided tours, visitors can view his personal belongings and photographs. The welfare of animals was one of his greatest passions, and this is evident throughout his house (he especially loved cats).

The currently exhibited "Gorey's Creatures ~ Real and Imagined" contains Mr. Gorey's original works including his many illustrations, his only pop-up book, and a three-dimensional accordion book.

The Edward Gorey House. *Illustration by T. M. Gray*, 2009.

Spooky New England Graves

H. P. Lovecraft's Grave Swan Point Cemetery

585 Blackstone Boulevard
Lot 5, Group 281
Providence, Rhode Island 02906
Phone: (401) 272-1314 (Call to verify hours)

Swan Point Cemetery is open during the summer, spring and fall from 6 a.m. - 7 p.m. and during the winter from 8 a.m. - 5 p.m. Admission Free.

To locate Mr. Lovecraft's grave, enter the Swan Point Cemetery through the front gates. Keep going straight until you come to Junction Avenue. Take a right onto Pond Avenue. When you reach the intersection with Avenue B, the large Phillips family monument will be straight ahead. H. P. Lovecraft's headstone is just behind it.

Although a prolific writer, H.P. Lovecraft did not die a wealthy man on March 15, 1937; for forty years no headstone marked his grave. In 1977, a group of his fans bought him a small granite headstone. His words "I AM PROVIDENCE" was engraved at the bottom of the stone.

On the night of October 13, 1997, someone tried to break into his grave. A security guard discovered a three-foot hole the next morning. The vandal was never caught...but whoever they were, they wouldn't have been successful in their gruesome endeavor. At the time of burial, a thick, concrete coffin liner was placed over Mr. Lovecraft's casket. This was not done to prevent his remains from being disturbed, but to save his grave from sinking into the ground over time.

Midnight Mary Evergreen Cemetery

769 Ella Grasso Boulevard,
New Haven, Connecticut 06519-1824
Phone: (203) 624-5505
Web: www.evergreencem.org/

Evergreen Cemetery is open during daylight hours only.

Mary E. Hart was born in New Haven, lived on Winthrop Avenue, and worked as a seamstress, a machine stitcher, and corset maker. In her 47th year, on October 15, 1872, around noon, Mary probably suffered what was then called an "apoplexy," what today is known as a stroke or cerebral embolism.

Her family presumed she had died and they buried her that afternoon. Mary's sister awoke at midnight after having a terrible nightmare in which she had heard Mary screaming in her grave. She alerted the rest of the family. Mary's coffin was disinterred, and when they opened the lid, poor Mary was truly dead. Evidently, she had been buried alive. Her bloodied fingers, torn fingernails and the scratches on the inside of the coffin, as well as her terrified grimace revealed her gruesome fate. She probably died of fright.

Her large, pink granite stone reads: "THE PEOPLE SHALL BE TROUBLED AND MIDNIGHT AND PASS AWAY" in ominous black letters over the rest of her epitaph: "At high noon just from, and about to renew her daily work, in her full strength of body and mind Mary E. Hart having fallen prostrate remained unconscious, until she died at midnight, October 15, 1872 Born December 16, 1824"

This gave birth to the legend of Midnight Mary. According to the stories, Mary's ghost is a "lady in white," a nocturnal hitchhiker on Winthrop Avenue, who suddenly vanishes before reaching her destination. In another urban legend, Mary was a witch with a cursed grave. Brave young souls often died after staying the night at her gravesite.

For well over a century, people have been spooked by the peculiar phrase on her grave. What did it mean? Was it some sort of warning or curse?

Not at all. Those familiar with scripture might recognize the passage from the Old Testament, Job 34:20, which in the King James Version (used at the time of Mary's death) reads: "In a moment shall they die, and **the people shall be troubled at midnight, and pass away**, and the mighty shall be taken away without hand." It was very common practice, especially in the 1800s, to engrave Bible verses on tombstones. Mary's family might have chosen this particular one because it speaks of the sovereignty of God who can take one's life at any given time.

To find Mary Hart's famous grave, enter Evergreen Cemetery through the main entrance. Evergreen Cemetery covers eighty-five acres, but her grave is easy to find. Just head straight to the very rear of the cemetery. Her grave is near the fence near Winthrop Avenue.

The Grave's Window
Evergreen Cemetery

Town Hill Road
New Haven, Vermont 05472
Phone: (802) 435-3296 (Evergreen Cemetery Associates)

The Evergreen Cemetery is open during daylight hours only.

Being buried alive was a real fear in the old days. A famous grave in Vermont testifies to this dreadful plight. It is known as "the grave with a window."

Dr. Timothy Clark Smith was born on June 14, 1821 at Monkton, Vermont. He worked as a clerk for the U.S. Treasury Department. After earning a medical degree in 1855, he became a staff surgeon in the Russian Army. Dr. Smith also served as U.S. Consul in Russia.

Dr. Smith passed away just after breakfast (not on October 31, Halloween, according to the legends) but on Saturday, February 25, 1893 at the Logan House hotel in Middlebury.

Because of his fear of premature burial, Dr. Smith was buried in a special crypt at Evergreen Cemetery in New Haven, Vermont. His son, Harrison, designed the two-room crypt. Dr. Smith's coffin was fitted with a window at eye level protected by a cement shaft and a 14-inch plate of thick glass.

According to the stories, in earlier times it was possible to peer down into the shaft and view Dr. Smith's remains. Allegedly, his coffin was outfitted with a hammer and chisel so he could escape from it on his own if he had to. Some say he was buried with a bell to ring and alert others if he awoke. Stairs (now capped) led down into the vault.

The site is not haunted. Today condensation and mold clouds the grave window, but that does not stop the curious from trying to peek inside.

The grave is a powerful witness to the fear of being buried alive…a fear that, despite modern embalming practices, remains entrenched in the human psyche. Even in recent times, escape devices for coffins were still being patented. It isn't unheard of to be buried with a cell phone.

Dr. Smith's crypt is not hard to locate; it's in the front of the cemetery on a large mound.

The Black Agnes
Green Mount Cemetery

P. O. Box 533 (mailing address)
State Street (physical address)
Montpelier, Vermont 05601
Phone: (802) 223-5352
Web: www.central-vt.com/web/grmount/

Green Hope Cemetery is open daily during daylight hours.

Green Mount Cemetery was dedicated in 1855 as a thirty-five-acre burial ground in Montpelier.

Legends surround a somber bronze statue seated on the back of a gravestone in Montpelier's Green Mount Cemetery. Despite its obvious male appearance, the statue is called "The Black Agnes." (It's not actually black, but green due to weathering.) It is a sculpture named *Thanatos*, the Greek personification of Death, by Karl Bitter. The inscription of the statue reads the final lines of *Thanatopsis* by poet William Cullen Bryant:

> "Thou go not like the quarry slave at night scourged to his dungeon but sustained and soothed by an unfaltering trust.
> Approach thy grave like one who wraps the drapery of his couch about him and lies down to pleasant dream."

According to the legends, it guards the grave of a murder victim, and those who sit upon the statue's lap are destined for three strokes of very bad fortune. Some risk-takers, again according to stories, have lain in the arms of the statue at midnight and have died within a week.

The statue of *Thanatos* sits at the grave of Montpelier businessman John Erastus Hubbard. Mr. Hubbard was born in 1847 and died from liver cancer on July 17, 1899. While not a murder victim (as the stories say), Mr. Hubbard was vilified in his later years in a fall from public grace. Despite this, he donated thousands of dollars for the Gothic Chapel-Vault building and cemetery gatehouse.

The legend of Black Agnes may have been propagated by his foes.

Green Mount Cemetery, however, is not without its ghosts.

The impressive statue of "Little Margaret" Pitkin (who died at age 6 in 1899) was created based on her photograph. Because of this, she is sometimes mistaken for the ghost of a girl reportedly seen walking to, and melding with, the statue of her mother.

That ghost girl supposedly haunts the monument of Martin M. and Fanny (Hubbard) Kellogg (Fanny was a biological aunt to John E. Hubbard with the Thanatos statue). The monument is a statue depicting a seated mother reading to her kneeling daughter. One major flaw with the story: Martin and Fanny died childless. Although they lived in New York City, they left their entire estate to the town of Montpelier. Contention arose when John Hubbard contested the will and thus gained control of their estate. The ghost girl, if she exists at all, is *not* the Kellogg's daughter.

That is not to say, however, that there aren't ghosts at Green Mount Cemetery. Although I do my best to debunk them, I do believe in ghosts, and a cemetery without them would be a rare find. At any rate, Green Mount Cemetery is well worth a visit just to see the beautiful monuments.

Thanatos by Karl Bitter. *Photo by Ferdinand Schevill*, 1917.

Guided tours of the cemetery are available by contacting the superintendent or cemetery director.

Bucks Monument

Main Street (Route 1)
Bucksport, ME 04416

Maine's most famous "gravestone" can be easily seen from Route 1 in Bucksport. While not actually a headstone, it is a monument for the founder of Bucksport, Colonel Jonathan Buck, buried several feet away.

Colonel Buck was born February 20, 1719, in Woburn, Massachusetts, and was commander at Fort Pownal in present-day Stockton Springs. During the American Revolution, he became Colonel of the 5th Militia Regiment of Lincoln County. The British forced him to flee to what is now Bucksport; from there he traveled by land to Haverhill, Massachusetts. After the war, he returned to Maine and founded the settlement of Bucksport. He became a Justice of the Peace before his death in March 1795.

In 1852, Colonel Buck's descendants erected the monument on Oak Hill…and about fifty years after that, stories about the man began to circulate because of a peculiar mark that appeared on the face of the monument.

The mark clearly resembles a human leg ending in a pointed foot.

In 1902, the September issue of *The New England Magazine* published an article by J. O. Whittmore titled, "The Witch's Curse, a Legend of an Old Maine Town," which discredits the stories circulating about Colonel Buck. Mr. Whittmore ends by stating, "…the legend was made to fit the foot and not the foot to fit the witch's curse."

It did little to quell the rumors that persist to this day.

In one of the stories, during the war, a Native American woman who went by the Franco-Christianized name "Jacquelyn" aided Colonel Buck. When she asked for payment after tending to his sick and injured men, Colonel Buck had none to give. She then put a curse on him, and he in turn accused her of witchcraft and saw that she was put to death.

Another story concerns a condemned witch named Ann Harraway who swore to "dance upon Buck's grave." Some versions paint her as the mother of Colonel Buck's illegitimate son. Supposedly, Ann was burned at the stake and the son ran away with a piece of her leg. (Another stain on the Buck monument resembles a heart, hence the legendary love affair.)

The major problem with the witch's curse stories lies in the period in which they supposedly occurred. In Colonial America, no records exist of witches being burnt at the stake. Maine had certain ties to the witch hunts, but there were no witches executed in Maine. There exists absolutely no documentation of women accused of witchcraft, let alone executed for it, around the time of the American Revolution in Maine.

Purportedly, Colonel Buck's heirs had the front of the monument sanded and cleaned, but like any good curse, it just kept coming back. Over the years, people from all over the world have come to Bucksport to view the leg on the stone. For those who take a closer look, the nearby plaque states Colonel Buck was "an honorable, industrious man," as well as being a Patriot and founder of Bucksport.

This leg-shaped stain has inspired stories about Bucksport's founder for over 150 years. *Courtesy Tom Gray, 2007.*

UFOs

Strange objects in the skies have been reported in New England since the early Colonial days. One of the earliest documented sightings took place in November 1896 at the Portsmouth Naval Shipyard, witnessed by guards who shot at the airship as it passed overhead.

Similar sightings were reported in 1909 in Willimantic, Connecticut and Providence, Rhode Island, and well into the mid-1940s in Belfast and South Portland, Maine. Such sightings occurred well before the Roswell incident, "Martian mania," and the sci-fi films of the 1950s. As of 1947, they were called airships, flying discs, and flying saucers until 1952, when the U.S. Air Force coined the term "UFO" (Unidentified Flying Object).

Many current investigators prefer the term Unidentified Aerial Phenomenon (UAP) to describe UFOs, as some cases are, in all likelihood, meteors or man-made aircraft, but for traditional purposes, this book will refer to them as UFOs.

Statistically, Boston, Massachusetts has seen more UFOs than any other New England location, followed by Providence, Rhode Island and Portsmouth, New Hampshire. Fireballs, lights and spheres are not included in these sightings of actual aircraft. Most aircraft reported are round or disc-shaped, however, some are crescent-shaped, triangular, cigar or cylindrical-shaped in metallic colors from black to silver and ranging in size from several meters across to 100 feet or more. Most are silent and have lights either along the rims or on the bottom landing surfaces.

Very few UFO occupant sightings have been reported, but these range in description from the "Nordic" (humanlike) to the bulb-headed, large-eyed Grey aliens, lizard men, or insect people. The many speculations concerning alien agenda are varied, but the most popular belief is that they appear to be conducting scientific research on our planet. Abductees have claimed to have tissue and hair samples taken from them, as well as sperm, ova, and unborn fetuses. Some believe aliens are involved in hybrid reproduction. It stands to reason that if different races of aliens exist, each group would have its own agenda. Whether or not they have our best interests in mind is anyone's guess. We know, from our own history on this planet, that strong, technologically-advanced cultures decimate weaker, "primitive" cultures. If we are being visited by beings from other planets, we are the weaker "primitive" culture.

If this is the case, why haven't we been wiped out? Several theories try to answer that question:

A. Because they are the future *us*. And if the past is destroyed, the present *and future* no longer exists.

B. Because they need us. We can fulfill something, which is lacking in them, perhaps on a genetic level.

C. Because Planet Earth is special, a kind of living museum. They may be bound by universal laws not to destroy life here.

D. Because UFOs are man made and not of extra-terrestrial origin.

Personally, I don't know. It's my best guess that some UFOs are created by the military, and some are not. I do believe the Earth is a very special planet, and that there must be others like it in the universe. I've seen what can only be described as a UFO, but I've never been aboard one or met the occupants.

There are those who have, however, and these are their accounts:

The Hill Abductions

The most famous case of alien abduction involved Betty and Barney Hill, who were taken aboard a spacecraft on September 19, 1961, at Indian Head, New Hampshire. The Hills were an interracial couple living in Portsmouth; Barney worked for the U.S. Postal Service and Betty was a social worker. On their way home from Niagara Falls, along Route 3 south of Lancaster, New Hampshire, they spotted a UFO in the night sky. Barney stopped the car, got out and peered at it through his binoculars.

Before reaching the Flume (33 miles from Lancaster), they noticed the UFO was closer, darting back and forth in the sky. They stopped a few miles later at Indian Head; Barney got out and looked at it again with the binoculars. The craft was large, disc-shaped, had multi-colored lights and rows of windows.

In its lit-up windows, he could see several occupants inside, but then the UFO moved closer. Betty screamed and Barney jumped back into the car. Driving away, they heard beeping sounds from the craft.

After driving thirty-five miles southward to Ashland, they heard the beeping sounds again. They noticed the loss of two hours, time that could not be accounted for. The Hills arrived home around 5 a.m. on September 20. Concerned about radiation from the UFO, they put their belongings from the car onto their back porch. Barney noticed the tops of the toes of his shoes were scuffed. When Betty took off her dress that morning, she noticed it was covered in pink-colored powder. Her earrings were missing and she wondered how she'd lost them.

For Betty, the nightmares began nine nights later . . . Strange dreams in which aliens (the Grey-type) brought them aboard their craft and conducted medical experiments on her and Barney. At first, Barney assumed his wife was just having a series of bizarre, vivid dreams; he had no idea at the time that PTSD (Post Traumatic Stress Disorder) sometimes produces series nightmares.

Under hypnosis, the Hills were able to recall their lost time. Humanoid aliens blocked the road and took the Hills to a landed UFO. Betty and Barney were brought to separate rooms aboard the craft. There they were stripped and made to lie down upon tables. Medical experiments were conducted.

According to Betty, under hypnosis, she could communicate with an alien and asked where he was from. He showed her a location on a "Star Map," and later Betty drew as much as she could remember of the map. Marjorie Fish researched Betty's map, which she found to line up with a certain portion of the sky. The alien indicated that he was from Zeta Reticuli.

About two months after their abduction, the Hills returned to the site to see if the location could trigger memories. When they returned home, they found a pile of leaves on their kitchen table. Under the leaves were the same earrings Betty had been wearing on the night of September 20.

Illustration of Barney Hill and the UFO that fateful September night, *Tom Gray, 2009*.

The Andreasson Abduction

Just after 6:30 p.m. on January 25, 1967, Betty Andreasson Luca, a mother of seven, was in the kitchen of her South Ashburnham, Massachusetts home when all the lights in the house suddenly blinked and went out. Red light flooded into the windows from outside. As Betty left the kitchen to comfort her children in the living room, her father looked out the kitchen window and saw five strangers "hopping" toward the house. If this wasn't weird enough, they didn't stop to knock at the door but walked straight *through* it.

They communicated telepathically with the family inside the house; they didn't hop but appeared to float. After putting Betty's children into a state of frozen consciousness, they released one of her daughters to show Betty that her children were safe. Betty was then brought outside to the spacecraft in her backyard.

This spacecraft joined with a mother ship where Betty was physically examined and subjected to bizarre tests involving strange equipment. She was returned to her family four hours later and after releasing the family from their trances, the aliens departed.

Betty was a devout Christian who believed her abduction had spiritual significance, but a decade would pass before her experience would be fully investigated. In January 1978, the first investigation was completed and the results were published in a 528-page document.

The document contains information told to Betty by her abductors, such as grey aliens are actually human fetuses harvested from humans and put inside artificial wombs where they are grown to maturity, and that Jesus Christ was returning soon. Her experience with her abductors, overall, was quite positive.

The Lake Champlain Abductions

On the late afternoon of August 7, 1968, at the Buff Ledge Camp on Lake Champlain just north of Burlington, Vermont, Michael Lapp and Janet Cornell were taking a break on the boat dock. Michael worked in camp maintenance; Janet was a water ski instructor.

Suddenly, a bright light appeared in the sky, which turned out to be a flying saucer. It dropped three smaller lights from beneath it and disappeared into the sky. Meanwhile, the smaller lights danced over the lake, zigzagging and looping in the air. Then they moved closer to Michael and Janet.

These objects made a triangular formation, but two pulled back as the front one approached the boat dock. It flew over them, shot up into the sky out of sight, then reappeared, tilted to one side and plunged into the water of the lake.

When it re-emerged from the depths and back into the air, the craft approached Michael and Janet, who could see two humanoids within its transparent cupola. Michael suddenly slapped his knee and watched as one of the aliens did the same thing. As it moved, then hovered overhead, the spacecraft emitted a beam so bright Michael could see the bones in his hand. He grabbed Janet and they landed on their backs on the boat dock.

The next thing they knew, Michael and Janet were sitting in the dark on the dock. Michael watched as the UFO soared into the sky, lights flashing. Janet seemed to be in a trance.

Ten years later, Michael underwent regressive hypnosis where he recalled his body being physically lifted by a beam emitted by the UFO. He was taken to a mother ship, where he saw Janet on an examination table. According to him, the aliens looked exactly alike (Grey-types) and they conveyed to him that they wanted peace on Earth and their mission was to bring human life "to other places." Janet also underwent hypnosis and recalled lying upon a cold table.

Others witnessed the lights over Lake Champlain at the Buff Ledge Camp that evening, and at least two of them were abducted by UFOs that same summer.

The Allagash Abductions

On August 21, 1976, three campers on the Allagash Wilderness Waterway in Maine: college students Chuck Rak, Charlie Foltz, Jim and Jack Weiner set up camp on Eagle Lake. That night they built a bonfire on the bank of the lake and went night fishing in their canoe. While on the lake, they noticed a UFO a few hundred yards away over the trees. It was large, around eighty feet in diameter, moving and changing colors.

Charlie shone his flashlight at it and the UFO moved toward them. Curiosity turned to terror as all four began paddling frantically to shore, hoping the craft would turn away. It didn't. Suddenly a cone-shaped ray of light beamed down upon them.

Then they were back at shore in their canoe near a circle of ashes and dying embers that had been their bonfire. The UFO was rising higher in the air, then flew away. To their estimation, they must have lost several hours; the fire had been burning brightly only moments before, and now its fuel of dry logs was totally spent. None of the four remembered anything that happened after the beam of light engulfed them; but strangely, they didn't feel like talking about it as they packed up and returned home.

Then the nightmares started. Jack experienced a series of terrible dreams of being examined by aliens with large heads and lidless eyes. He saw his friends in these dreams as well. He didn't know it at the time, but the others were suffering similar nightmares.

Twelve years later, Jack's twin brother Jim attended a UFO conference hosted by author Raymond Fowler, (now former) investigation director of MUFON (Mutual UFO Network). He spoke to Mr. Fowler and told him about the UFO he and his friends had seen at Eagle Lake. He also mentioned the beam of light and the missing time.

All four men agreed to undergo regressive hypnosis, the outcome of which was that they were abducted from their canoe that night, and while aboard the spacecraft, subjected to medical examinations. They drew pictures of the examination room, the medical instruments and the aliens who used them. They also took and successfully passed lie detector tests.

Much has been written about these famous cases, and more information can be easily researched in books, movies and magazines on the subject. (I highly recommend Raymond Fowler's books.)

The similarities of the New England abductions are intriguing:

- Occurring at sunset or night
- Most occurred in autumn
- Sighting of a bright light or UFO
- Several abductees taken at once
- Missing time

- Samples taken from abductees
- Strange marks left on bodies
- Similar descriptions of the aliens and their space craft
- Similar drawings provided by the abductees
- Lie detector tests passed

Arguments against these cases concern the abductees' stories enhanced under hypnosis, and the fact that lie detectors are not always one hundred percent accurate, but nothing so far can account for the amount of time lost by the abductees.

Illustration of the Allagash Abductions, *T. M. Gray, 2009.*

Spheres and Crop Circles

Spheres, lights, and fireballs are other phenomenon seen in the skies of New England. These come in colors ranging from blue, green, yellow, orange, red, purple, and white. Some spheres have been reported as having a metallic color. Interestingly, many seen have been described as suddenly changing direction, or floating slowly, then speeding off.

Some, of course, are probably ball lightning, as in the case of purple fireballs reported during a blizzard in Bass Harbor, Maine on February 13, 1853. Fireballs came into homes through doors, windows and chimneys. Several residents were injured by contact with the fireballs; one man, a sea captain, was lifted from his feet and thrown back several feet by one. Others were "electrized," [sic] their arms, hands, and feet going instantly numb. Fortunately, no one was killed.

One lightning bolt in this storm struck the ground and made a deep crater. From there, the electricity went outward in four directions through frozen soil, creating tunnels. One of the longest of these tunnels measured 370 feet in length and was at least 4 feet wide.

However, lightning cannot account for all fireballs, lights, and spheres, as some occur on cloudless, sunny days as well as starlit nights. Some people believe these may actually be extraterrestrial probes. Some spheres certainly tend to act that way, moving about as if measuring or examining things. Yet others think these phenomena could be unclassified life forms that exist in the atmosphere. (It may be just as possible that they could be both probes and life forms.) Whatever these may be, they *should not* be touched, as there are several accounts of people being blistered and burnt by them.

Just after midnight on August 4, 2002, several residents watched a light orb bouncing over a hayfield at Gardiner, Maine, accompanied by a "metallic-like noise." Hours later, crop circles in the hayfield were discovered. UFORC (National UFO Reporting Center) was notified, along with the BLT Research Team, Inc. of Cambridge, Massachusetts, a scientific group that investigates crop circles.

Lights have been seen over fields before in conjunction with crop circles and serious research is ongoing in these phenomena.

What should you do if you see a UFO?

- First, try to rule out every other possibility: Could it be a plane, bird, weather balloon, kite, meteor, or man-made satellite?
- Document the date, time, and location.
- Observe direction the object is moving.
- Take note of all colors, lights, shapes, and sounds associated with the object.
- Weather conditions at time of sighting.
- Size of object at arm's length.
- If possible, take a photograph or get a video of the object.

Sightings can be reported at:

MUFON (Mutual UFO Network) www.mufon.com

UFORC (National UFO Reporting Center) www.uforc.com

UFOWATCH www.ufowatch.com

FUFOR (Fund for UFO Research) www.fufor.com

NICAP (National Investigations Committee on Aerial Phenomena) www.nicap.org

Pilots, air traffic controllers or radar operators should report their sightings to:

NARCAP (National Aviation Reporting Center on Anomalous Phenomena) www.narcap.org

Law enforcement officers and scientists are encouraged to report their sightings to:

CUFOS (Citizens Against UFO Secrecy) www.cufos.org

New England's Vampires

When one thinks of vampires and New England, nightmarish visions of Stephen King's *Salem's Lot* and *Dark Shadow's* Barnabus Collins may come to mind...but in reality, the true story of the vampire of the American Northeast is far darker. Graveyards' iron fences and locked crypts were not put there to prevent vandalism, but to keep the dead *inside*.

The vampire of New England was born of desperate tradition, akin to the original vampires of Romania and Transylvania in the plague-ridden Dark Ages. Far removed from the romanticized vampire with pearly fangs and a sweeping cloak, the New England vampire was a real person who succumbed to a wasting disease such as "consumption," or "the White Death," what we now call pulmonary tuberculosis.

Vampirism was suspected only after several members a family died from the same disease. At the time, the term "vampire" was seldom used to describe the spreader of the disease. (One exception is the gravestone of Simon Whipple Aldrich, which *does* mention the word "vampire.") It is very likely no local terms existed for what had become of these unfortunate dead. The nearest word that fits today is: *Nosferatu, the plague bringer*.

Consumption, aka Tuberculosis, did indeed *appear* vampiric in nature; in many cases, its victim awoke in the night barely able to breathe, with fits of coughing, which often brought up blood. As anyone suffering with a cold knows: The symptoms always worsen at night. In the case of tuberculosis, the sufferer grew increasingly weak and pale as the disease wore on...and always, by night, the coughing worsened until death.

New England vampire tradition was famous prior to the first major publication introducing the vampire to the general public: Bram Stoker's *Dracula* (1897). Discovered among Mr. Stoker's papers were clippings from the *Providence Journal* about Mercy Brown of Exeter, Rhode Island. If the New England vampire inspired Bram Stoker, the same can be said for Rhode Island's favorite son, H.P. Lovecraft. "The Shunned House" (October 1924) tells his own version of the vampire.

The Nosferatu-type vampire, however, does have remarkable similarities to the colonial view of witchcraft, whereas it was believed a witch could inflict physical harm upon others at night without leaving his/her bed. Using an "astral" body and leaving the physical one behind, it was believed the witch could roam at will, therefore, any reliable alibi in a witchcraft trial was seldom accepted.

The same can be said of the New England Nosferatu, whose grave remained undisturbed since burial. Like the witch, this vampire traveled in his/her astral body, returning home at night, to the bedsides of beloved parents, brothers and sisters. And once there, they fed.

Those ill with disease usually became sicker, quite literally wasting away. Usually, a heartsick parent made the difficult choice to do what had to be done in order to save a remaining child. What is unthinkable in this day and age must have been equally horrific for them. Stephen Staples in his 1796 petition before a Cumberland, Rhode Island town council referred to the practice as "an experiment." Small wonder they had no words for it!

The gruesome tradition involved exhuming and examining the corpse of the suspected "feeder." If decay was found to be too prolific, another corpse was dug up, then another, until one was discovered showing significant "signs of life." Some of these signs were: fluid blood in the tissues or organs (especially the heart), hair or nails that had lengthened, reposition in the coffin, a bloated abdomen, blood or fluid in the mouth, etc. (One must remember that before embalming became standard, being buried alive did occur, and this would certainly account for a body shifting within its coffin. The body often would be moved as a coffin was taken from the ground. Bodily fluids coagulate, then thin as they break down, which might have accounted for the appearance of fresh blood.

The Vampire. *Philip Burne Jones, 1897.*

After death, flesh pulls back from the fingers, giving the nails a longer appearance, and depending on temperature, the age of corpse, and whatever entailed a last meal, there may be abdominal bloating. The common people of this era had little knowledge of the human decaying process; concerning physical death, they believed only what they could see.)

To prevent someone from returning from the grave, the dead had to be buried facedown, and a stake through the heart had to literally pin them to the ground. Few families, however, were willing to do that, for the godly were buried face up in expectation of Resurrection Day. To do otherwise could jeopardize the soul.

Once the feeder/vampire corpse was determined, its heart had to be cut out. Back then, it was believed that the heart, not the mind, was the seat of human soul. The heart was then roasted to ashes, the ashes were then mixed into a tea, and this tea was given to the afflicted family members to drink. Anthropologists refer to this practice as "medical cannibalism."

Sometimes the sick recovered, sometimes not. If they died, it was said it was because this "cure" had not been applied soon enough. If they lived, it may have been because they would have beaten the disease anyway, but the power of belief may have aided in the cure. At any rate, it was an experience they did not care to remember, let alone discuss.

Grave Digger. *Viktor Vasnetsov, 1871.*

Mercy Lena Brown

Historic Cemetery #22

Off Victory Highway, Rte. 102
(Behind the Chestnut Hill Baptist Church)
Exeter, Rhode Island 02822

West Greenwich resident, Nellie Vaughn has been thought by some to have been a vampire, due in part to a story in school, and because her gravestone bore the inscription: "I am waiting and watching for you."

Nellie died from pneumonia on March 31, 1889. Mercy Lena Brown succumbed to tuberculosis in January 1892. Both girls died at age 19. Like Mercy, Nellie's body was exhumed several months after her death. But the similarities stop there. Nellie's grave was moved in order to bring her from the family farm on Robin Hollow Road to the new cemetery at Plain Meeting House Road. Her epitaph meant only that she's in Heaven, watching over her loved ones, waiting to be reunited with them (which surely has happened by now). Rest assured, she is *not* a vampire; she doesn't wait and watch for YOU!

Part of Nellie's legend is that no grass grows on her grave. This is absolutely untrue. If you did not know *exactly* where her grave was, you would have a hard job finding it. It is not the large crypt in the middle; Nellie never had a crypt; she had a headstone *once* but it had to be removed for safekeeping. Sadly, this cemetery has seen its share of vandals. In the past, gravestones have been defaced and knocked over; the crypt was broken into, and on the Halloween night of 1993, a coffin was unearthed. Visitors are still welcome during the day, but this cemetery is closed at night.

The case of Mercy Lena Brown of Exeter is another story.

In December 1883, Mary Eliza Brown, a mother of six, died of consumption. Her husband, George, was a farmer and got by with the help of their daughters: dressmaker Mary Olive, Annie, Mercy Lena, Hattie, and Jennie. Their son, Edwin, was working in Wickford as a store clerk. Then Mary Olive contracted the disease that took her mother's life. She died in July 1884. Seven years passed.

Then Edwin fell sick. George recognized the symptoms, and worried for the outcome. Knowing this was consumption, the doctor advised Edwin to go to Colorado Springs, for the curative mineral waters there.

While her brother was out west, Mercy Lena fell ill to the disease, and soon after died in the January of 1892. The ground was too frozen for burial so her corpse had to stored in the crypt until Spring. That was about the time Edwin returned home.

It was not a happy homecoming; in all likelihood, 24-year-old Edwin had come home to die. Even with his young bride by his side, his health had declined. It is not known to this day who proposed that they make one last, desperate attempt to try to save Edwin, but it probably wasn't George's idea. According to a letter to the Editor of the *Pawtuxet Valley Gleaner* dated March 25, 1892, it wasn't the brainchild of Dr. Harold Metcalf of Wickford, either.

George stayed home with Edwin during the exhumations. First the coffin of mother Mary Eliza Brown was unearthed and its contents examined by the reluctant doctor. He found only skeletal remains. Mary Olive's body, like that of her mother, had been reduced to bones.

There must have been a few gasps when Mercy Lena's coffin was pried open. Some said her position had shifted; she was not lying flat on her back, but had turned in the grave. Her flesh was not decomposed, so her heart was removed and examined. Dr. Metcalf remarked that finding blood in the heart of the newly-deceased was common enough. Clearly, he did not believe she was feeding on her brother, but he was unable to convince anyone else.

Mercy Lena's heart and lungs were reduced to ashes on a nearby rock. These ashes were taken to the Brown house and mixed into water as a cure for Edwin. He died two months later on May 2, 1892. Certainly, it cannot be said they didn't try to save him!

Mercy was reburied in her grave in the Historic Cemetery #22. The cemetery is open all year during daylight hours. Some, including Brown relatives, have claimed to see a blue, glowing orb near Mercy's grave.

Le Vampire from Les Tribunaux secrets. *R. de Moraine, 1864.*

Sarah Tillinghast

Historical Cemetery #EX014

Forest Hills Drive
Exeter, Rhode Island 02822

Stukeley "Snuffy" Tillinghast was another farmer in Exeter. He lived in Pine Hill and had a large apple orchard. By all accounts, he was a hard-working, prosperous man, and was nicknamed "Snuffy" because the coat he wore was butternut brown. By 1789, Snuffy and his wife, Honor Hopkins-Tillinghast (married 22 Nov 1762 in West Greenwich), had 15 children:

Anna (Northup) b. 26 May 1768 in W. Greenwich, d. 9 Nov 1835
Amos b. 23 Oct 1764 in Exeter
Stephen b. 13 Jan 1766 in Exeter, d. 8 Jul 1845
Amey (Whitford) b. 29 Oct 1767 in Exeter, d. bef 9 Jul 1818
Honor (Reynolds) b. 24 May 1769 in Exeter, d. 26 Feb 1866 in Richmond, RI
Pardon b. 3 Feb 1771 in Exeter, d. 1854
*Hannah b. 26 Dec 1772 in Exeter, d. 1800
Stukeley, Jr., b. 29 Jun 1774 in Exeter, d. 13 Mar 1848
Mary b. 21 Jan 1776 in Exeter, d. 1863
*Sarah b. 10 Oct 1777 in Exeter, d.1799
*Ruth b. 29 Jan 1780 in Exeter, d. 1799
*Aunstis b. 18 Jan 1782 in Exeter, d. 1799
Clark b. 17 Apr 1784 in Exeter, d. 11 Nov 1832
*James b. 21 Aug 1786 in Exeter, d. 1799
Reuben b. 1789 in Exeter, d. 6 Nov 1872

(*Those dying of Consumption)

Then one night in 1799, Snuffy had a terrible dream in which half the trees in his orchard died. This caused him to wake up in a sweat, but his wife soothed him, and he soon fell back asleep. Still, he wondered what his dream meant. The next morning, he checked his orchard and everything seemed fine.

He might have forgotten his nightmare if not for his 22-year-old daughter, Sarah. She fell sick, and the diagnosis was a virtual death sentence. It was a case of "galloping" consumption, what we now know as "Acute Pneumonic Phthisic Wasting Disease." It leads to death quickly, usually in four to eight weeks, by quite literally *consuming* its victim with night-sweats, high fevers, rapid emaciation, a violent, dull cough that brings up thick, green expectoration, followed at last by the lungs hemorrhaging blood. It can strike at any age, but it often targets children and young adults.

Just after Sarah died, 19-year-old Ruth fell sick with the same dreadful symptoms. But this girl told her parents that every night Sarah would come to her bed and sit down on some part of her body. Hannah, Aunstis and James became sick, too.

According nineteenth-century historian Sidney Rider, Snuffy Tillinghast had no idea what the dream meant for a long time. But when six (most sources say four/five) of his children died of consumption, one right after another, and a seventh child was taken ill, he realized that the apple orchard in his dream symbolized his own children.

Every sick Tillinghast child had complained about their older sister Sarah sitting on them at night. By now their mother was ill with the same sickness, and she also claimed nocturnal visitations by Sarah. Desperate to save his remaining family, Snuffy spoke with his neighbors on what to do.

Among them, someone knew of a possible cure. Where they had learned of it, no one knows. Perhaps from an indentured servant or slave? Or from an old story they'd heard long ago? At any rate, according to Dr. Bell, those neighbors by name of Mooney, Reynold, Wilcox, Whitford, Gardner, and others, helped to exhume the Tillinghast children. (Why they didn't *start* with Sarah is beyond me!)

Each child's corpse was decayed, except for that of Sarah. "It was clear at once to these astonished people that the cause of their trouble lay there before them," wrote Rider. She was, according to the historian, in "remarkable condition… The eyes were opened and fixed. The hair and nails had grown, and the heart and the arteries were filled with fresh red blood."

After reburying the other children, and removing Sarah's heart, they burned it to ashes on a rock in front of the Tillinghast house. The cure was administered, and Mrs. Tillinghast recovered (she died December 2, 1831, at age 86), but, according to Rider, the seventh child died. "Thus was the dream of Stukeley fulfilled."

Dr. Bell conducted some genealogical research of the Tillinghast family and found records of a Stukeley in the area who had fourteen children. Four of them died in 1799.

Sarah Tillinghast is buried with her family. The Tillinghast lot is twenty feet east of Forest Hills Drive off Victoria Highway. It is enclosed within a stonewall. The cemetery is open during daylight hours.

Nancy Young

Cemetery #FR142

Jenks Road
Foster, Rhode Island 02825

In 1827, another young lady fell ill with consumption. Nancy Young, eldest daughter of Captain Levi and Annie (Perkins) Young, had been "a very bright and intelligent girl." She died on April 6th, 1827, at the tender age of 19.

Just before Nancy's death, her sister Almira, "a very sprightly girl" became sick and it became clear she had consumption. Just after Nancy died, in the grip of fever's delirium, Almira told her father that Nancy had visited her and said her pain would soon end. Captain Young hired the best doctors to treat his daughters, but their efforts could not save either of them. Almira died on August 19, 1828 at age 17. The Young family of Foster, Rhode Island, was large and well liked, and when the two girls passed away, the entire town mourned their loss.

By the summer of 1828, two more of the Youngs' children became ill with the disease, and the good Captain requested that their friends and neighbors help him provide a means of prevention. Where he had heard of this solution, and who told him about it remains a mystery. Certainly, it shocked everyone, but they must have agreed to come to his aid, knowing but for the grace of God, the same fate could befall their own families.

Since Nancy was the first to die from consumption, her body would have to be exhumed and burnt, while the surviving family members gathered around and inhaled the smoky fumes.

It did not work as planned. Yes, her body was exhumed and burnt. And her family drew near to inhale the smoke.

And shortly after, five more of the Young children died. Only a son and two daughters escaped death by consumption.

Nancy Young is buried in the Young Lot. The cemetery is open during daylight hours.

Ruth Ellen Rose

Peace Dale, Rhode Island 02883

Ruth Ellen Rose died from consumption on May 12, 1874 at age 15. Her father, William G. Rose of Peace Dale, must have believed she was causing sickness among her siblings. It is said he exhumed her corpse and burned her heart in the hope of saving the lives of his remaining children. At this time, the outcome of their fates remains unknown.

An interesting twist to this case is that Ruth Ellen's stepmother, Mary Rose, was the great granddaughter of Stukeley Tillinghast. According to Dr. Bell, Mary would have been about age 26 when her grandfather Amos died, and likely knew the stories of how his siblings' graves had to be disinterred, their corpses exhumed, to stop the spread of consumption in the family. Hence, it is very likely that she may have offered this advice as a solution to her husband William.

Ruth Ellen Rose's grave has yet to be found.

Jullian Wright

Westerly, Rhode Island 02891

Shortly after Jullian Wright's death in 1704, a visitor at the cemetery heard Jullian calling out to him. Fearing that the young man, the youngest son of a Westerly, Rhode Island plantation owner, had been buried alive, he reported this to Jullian's father. No other sounds were heard, and the report was dismissed as grief.

That week, several servants and Jullian's sister, Anna, stated that Jullian was visiting them at night. It did not take long for each of these people to fall ill with consumption. Within several months, they were to the point of death, and Jullian was still visiting, so they claimed.

Under the circumstances, the Constable of Westerly allowed Jullian Wright's remains to be disinterred. The Constable's report preserved in the State Archives stated that Jullian's body was found "in perfect condition...and the lid to his coffin had been scratched to the point as a hole had been made."

After beheading the body, the heart was removed. The Constable found the corpse "gorged with the blood of its victims." The corpse was then turned over in its grave and a stake was driven through it to pin it to the ground. The boy's head and heart were duly burned to ashes, which were stirred into a tea for his sister and servants.

With exception of one servant who died, Anna Wright and the servants made a full recovery. The servant who died was an older woman who was buried as a precaution (facing downward and staked through the heart) "in proper manner as to insure the public safety." As of 2009, Jullian Wright's grave has not been located.

Abigail Staples

Historical Cemetery #CU017

Nate Whipple Highway
Cumberland, Rhode Island 02864

According to the Cumberland Town Council Records, Vol. 4, p.1: on February 8, 1796, Stephen Staples asked permission of the Cumberland Town Council to "try an Experiment." The experiment involved exhuming the corpse of his daughter Abigail, who died from consumption in 1785. He told them that his daughter, Livina (Staples) Chase, wife of Stephen Chase, had consumption. He felt she would die if he didn't do something. He promised after "trying the Experiment," he would "bury the Body of the Said Abigail In a Deasent [sic] Manner[.]"

The town of Cumberland granted his request. It is unknown if the cure worked.

Abigail Staples is buried in the Staples Family Lot in Cumberland. Many of the gravestones here are unreadable.

Simon Whipple Aldrich

Union Cemetery Annex

Great Road
North Smithfield, Rhode Island 02824

Simon Whipple Aldrich was born about 1814 and died May 6, 1841. The inscription on his gravestone reads: "Altho' consumption's **vampire** grasp hath seized thy mortal frame…" We'll never know how the epitaph ended; half the headstone is missing.

The Walton Family

Hopeville, Connecticut 06351

In November 1990, two young boys were sliding down a gravel bank when one unearthed what he first assumed was an old coconut. It turned out to be a human skull. Another skull was found nearby, and by this time, the boys' imaginations must have run wild. Was this the site of a grisly murder? One of the boys hurried home to tell his mother.

She didn't believe him, so he went back and fetched the skull to show her. She called the police…then, no doubt made him scrub his hands!

After an initial investigation, forensic researchers were called to the gravel slope. They determined the site was that of an old abandoned family graveyard, and because of erosion, the graves had to be moved. There were twenty-nine corpses in all: six men, eight women, twelve children, and three babies. State Archaeologist Nick Bellantoni was stunned to find the dismembered skeletal remains of a man buried possibly as far back as the 1790s. Someone had taken great pains to arrange the remains in this coffin in a very peculiar way: severing the skull from the spine, turning it face down and placing it inside the upper rib cage. The two long femur bones were positioned in an "X" on the lower ribs just below the skull. Clearly someone had deliberately desecrated this corpse, but why? A study showed that his bones had been moved about five years after his death.

A study of the man's skeleton revealed that he had suffered from raging consumption. Buried nearby were the bodies of IB-46, a woman, and NB-13, a child. Since the initials on his coffin were JB-55, chances are, all three were relatives, perhaps members of the same family with a surname beginning with the letter "B." It can be assumed that J. B. died of consumption at age 55, possibly leaving a wife and child.

It is equally possible that several years later, his body was exhumed after some of his relatives fell sick with consumption. But suppose his heart had turned to dust?

By placing the bones in the skull and crossbone position is an old Northern European means of preventing a corpse from walking from the grave. If it was meant to save the lives of the woman, IB-46, or the child, NB-13, it did not work. Like J. B., both apparently died from consumption.

According to historians, the folks in this graveyard belonged to the Walton family. They moved to Connecticut from Massachusetts in 1690 and surviving family members left for Ohio sometime after 1830. It is not known where the Waltons of Hopeville were reinterred.

The Ray Family

Jewitt City Cemetery

Anthony Street
Griswold, Connecticut 06351

The Ray family lived in what was known as Jewitt City in Griswold. Henry B. Ray (1786-1849) and Lucy (Downing) Ray (1791-1861) had five children:

Henry Nelson, b. 1820 d. 1854
Lemuel Billings, b. 1821 d. 1845
James L., b. 1823 d. 1894
Elisha H. b. 1825 d. 1851
Adaline, b. 1827 d. 1897

In 1845, Lemuel was the first of the Ray family to contract deadly consumption and he died that March. Four years later, the father, Henry B. succumbed to the disease, and two years after that, Elisha fell ill with consumption and died as well.

In early May 1854, Henry Nelson Ray, was diagnosed with consumption. He was 35 years old, and his remaining family members must have decided they could lose no more sons in the prime of their lives. On the night of May 8th, with the help of their neighbors and friends, the graves of Lemuel and Elisha were opened, and the corpses of these brothers were burnt to ashes. Apparently, the father's grave went untouched.

The headstone of Henry N. Ray attests that these efforts failed to cure his consumption. He died in 1854. The Ray family lived just two miles from the Walton farm.

Janey D. Denitt

Barnstead, New Hampshire 03225

On September 3, 1820, a young preacher named Enoch Hayes Place left his home in Freewill, New Hampshire, to spread the word of God in Vermont. He kept a meticulous journal, and within two days, in Barnstead, New Hampshire writes of "a melancholy sight…as I never saw before."

He was referring to an event he attended on early Wednesday morning, September 5th. Enoch Place went with Esquire Hodgdon, George Denitt, a man named Adams, and other neighbors to exhume the grave of Janey D. Denitt, who had died more than two years earlier at age 21. She had suffered from consumption and now her father, George, was stricken with it.

Place describes the "melancholy sight" as Adams examined the "mouldy Specticle [sic]… There was but a little left except bones and part of the Vitals." No mention is made of burning or the administering of ashes.

From Barnstead, Enoch Place goes to Loudon, Vermont, where he learns more about the practice of raising the dead to heal the living:

They told him of a woman who had been dead eleven years, whose grave was exhumed by Shakers for similar purpose. Her corpse was reduced to bones, but from these remains grew eleven sprouts resembling the eyes of potatoes when left to grow. The thickest sprouts grew from her stomach, one out through the top of her skull, and a number of others "Stood upon the bone." Someone either intentionally or accidentally removed or "broke off" these sprouts, and died shortly thereafter. None of this did any good for the afflicted person.

The Spaulding Family

Dummerston Center Cemetery

East Dummerston, Vermont 05301

According to Dummerston historian David L. Mansfield, one of the old superstitions in the case of consumption among family members was that a root connected coffins underground, and once the root reached the next coffin, another family member would die. The only remedy was to exhume the corpse of the last one buried and burn the vital organs, thus destroying the root.

He claims that following this procedure, the daughter of the afflicted family in Dummerston "got well and lived many years." This daughter may have been a member of the Spaulding family, for he wrote: "…after six or seven of the family had died of consumption, another daughter was taken, it was supposed, with the same disease. It was thought she would die, and much was said in regard to so many of the family dying of consumption when they all seemed to have the appearance of good health and long life."

In his research, Dr. Bell found the Spaulding family of Dummerston had lost eight* of its members in less than 12 years to consumption:

Margaret (Lovell) Spaulding, mother, b. 1730 in Rhode Island d. 1 May 1827

*Lt. Leonard Spaulding, father, b. 27 Oct 1728 in Westford, MA d. 17 Jul 1788

*Reuben, b. 19 Nov 1756 in Westford, MA d. 20 Jan 1794 in Dummerston, VT

*Betsey (Stevens), b. 22 Jun 1758 in Westford, MA d. 2 Feb1790 in Dummerston

*Leonard, Jr., b. 14 Mar 1760 in Westford, MA d. 3 Sep 1792 in Dummerston, VT

*Mary (Lawton), b. 11 Oct 1761 in Putney, VT d. 12 May 1782 in Dummerston, VT

Sarah (Wilder), b. 19 Jul 1763 Westmoreland, NH d. 17 Sep 1841 Farmersville, NY

*John (twin), b. 13 May 1765 d. Mar 26 1793 in Dummerston, VT

*Timothy (twin), b. 13 May 1765 d. 13 Jun 1786 in Dummerston, VT

*Esther (twin), b. 7 April 1767 in Putney, VT, d. July 1783 in Dummerston, VT

Anna (twin) (Laughton), b. 7 Apr 1767 in Putney, VT d. 31 Jan 1849 Dummerston

*Josiah, b. 30/31 Mar 1772 d. Dec. 1798 in Dummerston, VT

Olive (1Wilson, 2Mixer), b. 17 Oct 1773 d. prob. Brattleboro, VT

(*Those dying of Consumption)

Lieutenant Spaulding was an American patriot and the first man in Dummerston to "shoulder his gun and start for Westminster for the fight of March 13, 1775." In the American Revolution, he gained a captain's commission, fought in the Battle of Bennington and was wounded in the battle of White Plains. For five years until his death, he represented Dummerston in the General Assembly.

No headstones mark the graves of Lieutenant Leonard Spaulding and his wife.

Rachel (Harris) Burton

Dellwood Cemetery?

2950 Route 7A
Manchester, Vermont 05254

Manchester historian John S. Pettibone claimed an eyewitness to the following events gave the following account to him.

In March 1789, Captain Isaac Burton married Rachel Harris, a young lady noted for her beauty. Not long after the exchange of vows, Rachel became sick, and the doctor's diagnosis was a death sentence: consumption. Despite every effort to save her, Captain Burton's bride succumbed to death in the February of 1790.

Surely the Captain mourned her death, and likely felt robbed of what life could have been for them had she lived. Perhaps his friends and family encouraged him to try to move on, to get past his grief. In January 1791, he met another bride at the altar. Her name was Hulda Powel, and while she lacked Rachel's delicate beauty, she was healthy and strong.

Not long after the wedding, Hulda became sick, and was soon diagnosed with consumption. The Captain must have been beside himself. Surely, this was a curse! By 1792, as her symptoms worsened, he would have moved Heaven and earth to spare her life! What may have been whispers in the village were now open suggestions: It may well be that a vampire was sucking the life out of Hulda. Everyone suspected this is what happened to Rachel.

Timothy Mead, the local blacksmith, and family friend believed vigorously that the death of Rachel and Hulda's sickness was the evil work of a demonic vampire, one who had for some unknown reason selected to victimize the wives of Captain Burton. Timothy suggested that they make a sacrifice to the Vampire in hopes that he would turn his attention away from Hulda.

Rachel was to be the sacrifice.

It is estimated that as many as 1,000 people: family, friends, and curious onlookers were present during the February thaw of 1793 when Rachel Burton's grave was opened. Her corpse was said to be in dreadful condition, but despite this, her heart, liver and lungs were removed, and burned in Mead's own blacksmith forge. The ashes were then fed to Hulda as cure. Some sources say the rest of Rachel's body was then burned, a sacrifice to the Demon Vampire.

Hulda Powel Burton finally succumbed to consumption on September 6, 1793. Isaac Burton is buried in the old section of the Dellwood Cemetery. As of 2009, Rachel Harris's grave has yet to be found.

Mr. Corwin

Cushing Cemetery?

Woodstock, Vermont 05091

The following story was published in early October 1890 in the *Boston Transcript* and in the *Vermont Standard*. The *Journal of American Folklore* published an article in 1889 by Jeremiah Curtin that contained an eyewitness account.

In the 1830s, a Woodstock man by the surname of Corwin died from consumption and was buried in the Cushing Cemetery. Not long after his death, his brother became ill with the disease. To save the ill brother, the town fathers decided that the grave of the dead Corwin be opened and the body exhumed to examine for signs of the supernatural.

Dr. Joseph Gallup, head of the Vermont Medical College, led the examination, and found that the "vampires heart contained its victim's blood." He must have come to this conclusion by reasoning that a corpse could not make blood on its own. It had to take blood from someone else by feeding upon them.

Evil of this magnitude required cleansing by fire. The village green was selected as a suitable place to carry out the task, and nearly everyone in town showed up to watch as Dr. Gallup and other doctors made a fire in the middle of the green beneath a large iron pot. In this, the heart of Corwin's corpse was burnt. The barely-living brother was then fed some of his brother's ashes mixed with the blood of a bull. The iron pot was buried in a deep hole and covered with a granite slab.

Afterwards, everything was sprinkled with bull's blood for purification.

It is unknown if the Corwin brother survived, as one writer put it: the disease *or* the cure. According to author and researcher Joe Nickell, there doesn't appear to be any Corwins on record buried in the Cushing Cemetery.

Frederick M. Ransom

South Woodstock, Vermont 05091

The Norman Williams Public Library of Woodstock has an unpublished, first-hand account dated about 1807. It reads as follows:

> "Frederick Ransom, the second son of my father and mother, was born in South Woodstock, Vermont, on June 16, 1797 and died of consumption February 14, 1817, at the age of about 20. He had a good education and was a member of Dartmouth College at the time of his death. My remembrance of him is quite limited as I was only three years [old] at the time of his death and I date my remembrance of anything at a visit of Dr. Frost to Frederick in his sickness. Keeping shy of the Doctor, fearing he would freeze me. [Dr. Frost. Cold, get it?]
>
> "It has been related to me that there was a tendency in our family to consumption, and that I, who now in 1894 am over 80 years old, would die with it before I was 30. It seems that Father shared somewhat in the idea of hereditary diseases and withal had some superstition, for it was said that if the heart of one of the family who died of consumption was taken out and burned, others would be free from it. And Father, having some faith in the remedy, had the heart of Frederick taken out after he had been buried, and it was burned in Captain Pearson's blacksmith forge. However it did not prove a remedy, for mother, sister, and two brothers died with that disease afterward."

There was indeed a Frederick M. Ransom, son of Richard and Elizabeth "Betsey" (Mather) Ransom of South Woodstock, Vermont. Frederick was a senior at Dartmouth College in 1817. According to Henry Swan Dana (*History of Woodstock, Vermont* [1889]), Frederick was "One of the most promising of all young men who were ever members of the (Library) Fraternity (established in 1815)...fitted for college in the North Village, as the Green was sometimes called, where he became a great favorite with all who knew him. Entering Dartmouth College, he there took a high stand as a scholar, and was much esteemed by all; but on account of failing health he was obliged to leave college during his last year and returned home, but died after a few week's illness."

Families Unknown

West Stafford, Connecticut

In the years between 1872 and 1888, a family with six daughters was afflicted with consumption. Five of the girls died quickly of the disease, and in order to save the remaining daughter, the graves of her siblings were disinterred. When the culprit was discovered, and the heart and lungs burnt, the sick girl recovered her health.

According to Tolland County historian, J. R. Cole, the Boston Health Board describes such a case that took place in West Stafford in 1872.

Plymouth, Massachusetts

An 1822 newspaper article relayed the tragic story of a Plymouth family of fourteen reduced to a mother and youngest son by consumption within the year of 1807.

Just weeks after the death of the 16-year-old daughter, the last remaining child, a son, began showing symptoms of consumption. The desperate mother consented to the opening of her 16-year-old's grave, the body exhumed, and examined, to be burnt if necessary to save the boy's life.

Five people, presumably the Plymouth Constable, a doctor, the gravediggers, and the surviving brother went to his sister's grave at sunrise. After prying open the lid of her coffin, and lifting the grave veil from her face, they found she was "lit up with the brilliancy of youthful health." Her cheeks were full, dimpled, alabaster pale. Her hair was thick and rich with color. Her large blue eyes were wide open, "had scarcely lost [their] brilliancy and the livid fullness of her lips seemed almost to say, 'loose me and let me go.'"

Despite the dark, seductive beauty of the corpse, her heart was cut out and burned, and her body turned over to face the ground for reburial. Despite partaking his sister's "curative" ashes, the boy died within two weeks. The poor mother lived only for a few more months thereafter. It is not known if she died from consumption; no doubt, she died with a broken heart.

Dr. Allen's patients

Saco, Maine

Dr. Henry Bowditch believed that consumption might be caused by living in cold, damp places. That would certainly explain why it was so prevalent in New England. Dr. J. L. Allen of Saco was one of Dr. Bowditch's correspondents, providing him with data on consumption cases and their relation to geography.

In one of his studies, Dr. Bowditch wrote that Dr. Allen noticed two ridges of land nearly identical except for the moisture in the soil. Almost every family living on the damper ridge was decimated by consumption while nearly all families living on the drier ridge escaped the disease. He adds, "In fact, in former times, the superstitious *frequently* had their friends, who had died of consumption, disinterred, and Dr. Allen invariably found the coffins filled with water, however shallow may have been the graves."

Apparently, exhumations were a frequent occurrence "in former times" in the Saco area, and were attended by at least one local doctor.

Penobscot County, Maine

In 1826, a family living in a town near Bangor was struck with consumption. Three of its members died soon after contracting the disease. According to an article in *The Bangor Whig and Courier*, "a woman of about 60 years of age," walked several miles to consult a Bangor doctor about his possible assistance in procuring the heart of one who'd died as, "…relief for her poor friend." However, the doctor refused and said he "did not believe in this resurrection business," and the helpful friend left "with a heavy heart, much aggrieved."

Apparently, without the doctor's help, the corpse of the last deceased sister was exhumed. The heart was extracted. A tincture was prepared from its ashes, and this was administered to the ill sister.

Medical cannibalism was by no means a tradition confined to old New England. The Papyrus Ebers of ancient Egypt contains a recipe for eyesight comprised of human brain and honey. According to the early accounts of Rome, the blood of gladiators was given as a tonic to cure epilepsy. During the Renaissance, powder from ground-up Egyptian mummies was used as an elixir for palsy and epilepsy. If applied externally, it was believed to heal wounds and sores, and could prevent bruising. Almost daily, King Charles II of Britain used a tincture of human skull mixed with wine and opium, prepared in his private laboratory at Whitehall. "Spirit of Skull," "King's Drops" or "English Drops" were then widely used and believed to cure epilepsy and headaches. At the time, one could easily purchase a human skull from any number of London apothecaries. As a cure for arthritis, Paris druggists sold Human "suet" "prepared with aromatic herbs." Such *suet* bought straight from the local executioner was said to be "of lesser quality."

Modern medicine has some very dark roots. Today we are careful to be ethical; we would not dream of using human corpses to cure diseases… yet miracles happen everyday with organ transplants from dead donors.

New England's Witchcraft Persecutions

Maine

Connecticut

New Hampshire

Massachusetts

Witchcraft was among the beliefs brought to the New World by early colonists and it took root in New England, where the rates of indictments of this "crime" were as much as twenty-five times higher and the rates of execution eight times higher than in England. The law against witchcraft was based on a Bible verse, Exodus 22:18: "Thou shalt not suffer a witch to live." In 1604, English law decreed it a capital offense.

By 1647, witchcraft was punishable by death in all the New England colonies. That year, America's first witch was executed in Hartford, Connecticut. Contrary to popular belief, not one of the condemned witches of the colonies was burned at the stake, as was the case in Europe. Most were hung from the gallows. One was pressed to death beneath weights.

The typical New England witch was a female, usually old, almost always poor, and had some personality flaw that made her a social outcast. She may have been alone, a widow, or her husband may not have been a power player in town politics. She stood out in a crowd. She may have been a midwife or a healer, having knowledge of herbs and folklore medicines. Certainly, not all people accused of witchcraft in New England were women or girls; there were a handful of men accused of witchcraft here as well. Men were more likely to be imprisoned or executed for the crime, less apt to be pardoned than women.

The witch was believed to be in league with the Devil, having signed his/her name in the Book of the Damned in trade for supernatural powers. One of the greatest of these powers was the ability to astral travel, to leave one's body asleep in bed and go out into the night to physically torment enemies or competitors. Another ability was to talk with animals and own a demon in the form of a familiar, usually a bird or a cat. The witch could put a curse or hex on someone or something, and it would happen. This could be verbal or just by giving "the evil eye." Horseshoes were nailed above doors, not so much for luck but rather in the belief they would prevent a witch from entering the premises.

The New England witch was unique in that he/she could have been *anyone*. From the scolding fishwife to the most pious churchgoer, the witch could have been a neighbor or friend, a relative, even one's own spouse, child, or parent. All it took was a single accusation to lead to an arrest. At trial, nearly every statement made by the accused was twisted. If the accused recited Bible verses, the jury was reminded that the Devil, too, knew scripture. A plea of not guilty almost always led to execution, whereas it was the God-given duty of the judge, jury, and executioner to "cleanse the soul" of the accused by taking their life. A guilty plea was accepted, and execution forgone if the guilty party gave the names of all others who were witches in their coven. Some people took this option, fearing for their lives, whereas others did not, remembering the Lord's commandment against bearing false witness against one's neighbor. For them, a physical death was better than risking damnation.

Arresting A Witch. *Howard Pyle, 1883.*

Thus, early New Englanders took Witchcraft very seriously, although occasionally, people were accused and charges brought against them for underhanded matters of personal gain, such as property. There were physical ways, of course, to determine a witch, but this involved stripping the accused person and having their entire body examined in front of the jury. Skin tags or "witch's teats" were sure signs of a witch, as it was believed these were where demons suckled. Birthmarks were another sign. So, too were sores or injuries, especially those hidden by clothing, not to mention warts and moles, even freckles.

Were any of the accused really witches? By definition of a witch, meaning one who makes use of magical spells and potions, hexes and the like, probably not. But these were superstitious times; nearly everyone believed in magic, and many practiced some form of it in their daily lives. For example, young girls would peel apples and look for the initials of a future husband in the fallen peel, some people could predict the future from the tea leaves left in the bottoms of their cups, many farmers would only sow or harvest on a certain phase of moon believing they'd have better luck with their crops. While none of this made them witches, per se, any of it could be used *against* them if they stood accused.

In 1703, Massachusetts law cast aside "Spectre Evidence," disallowing it in court cases. It was a step in the right direction. In 1728, Rhode Island made witchcraft a felony, "...whosoever shall be lawfully convicted thereof shall suffer the pains of death." King George II enacted the Witchcraft Act of 1735, which repealed witchcraft as a capital crime in both England and her colonies.

Many accused witches have been exonerated in later years, like Eunice "Goody" Cole of Hampton, New Hampshire and the many convicted in Salem, Massachusetts, while others like Mary Sanford of Hartford, Connecticut still wait for exoneration.

In Maine, several people were considered witches: Hannah Stover of Harpswell, Mary (Miller) Nasson, and Francis Trickey of York, "Lizzie" of Bowdoin, Barbara Houndsworth and Vera/Elvira of Belfast. No documentation or verification exists of any formal accusations brought forth against them, but because some are believed to have connections with haunted places, I researched their histories and wrote of my findings in my 2008 ghost hunter's guide: *Ghosts of Maine*. The following entries from Maine are not included in my previous book.

Los Caprichos Linda Maestra. *Francisco Goya, 1799.*

Maine

Goody Bailey

In 1659 at Spurwink, Old Falmouth (now Portland), Maine, a drunken preacher by name of Mr. Thorpe had appeared as a minister at Black Point, and boarded at the home of Goodman Bailey. When Goody Bailey informed him that drinking to excess was contrary to the Gospel of Christ, that he should reform or leave her house, he chose to depart.

Mrs. Bailey said she was going to travel to Casco Bay, an intended trip known to many. About that time, a cow belonging to Mr. Jordan of Spurnick died, and in this, Mr. Thorpe, who had been embarrassed by Mrs. Bailey, saw an opportunity for revenge.

Thorpe went to Jordan's man and told him the cow had been bewitched to death, and if they would lay the carcass in a place he should appoint, he would burn it and bring forth the witch. This was done, after all, who would disbelieve a preacher? The dead cow was laid by the path leading from Black Point to Casco, and burned. And who should come along, but Goody Bailey, on her way to Casco Bay.

Thorpe had her questioned for a witch, but fortunately, Mr. Jordan testified that his cow died by his servant's own neglect. This servant was more than willing to let Goody Bailey take the blame for the cow's death. Mr. Jordan had known of Mrs. Bailey's intended journey, and thus "unbridled the knavery and delivered the innocent."

A side note in *The New England Historical and Genealogical Register* adds: "Thorpe was presented to the court by Jordan and Jocelyn, in 1659, for "preaching unsound doctrine." Hale calls him a "drunken preacher"; Mrs. Bailey calls him a very bad man and drives him from her house; Jordan calls him a knave. Whence he came, whither he went into and out of this year of grace, 1659, we know not. This is all we hear of him. Unhappy memory!" (Mr. Hale may have had this from Mr. Jordan himself, but probably from his friend, Mr. John Phillips of Boston, with whom he had conversed on the subject of witchcraft, and who had, in that same year, bought an estate in the vicinity of Spurwink, at Falmouth.")

Daggett's Bewitched Horse

Henry Esensa had been a Hessian cavalry soldier, who moved to Broad Bay sometime after 1778. In or around 1813, he sold or traded a horse with Samuel Daggett. Henry's wife, Susannah (Rolfe) Esensa was said to have had the reputation "among a few ignorant people" of being a witch, and she wasn't particularly pleased with the trade. As the horse was led away to the town of Union, she was heard to remark that the animal had "always been a plague, and would never do the Daggetts any good."

The horse did not turn out to be a plague. However, it seemed no rope could keep him fettered. He was constantly getting loose in the stable. Samuel Daggett called upon his friend Captain John Tobey to see what he could do to help.

Captain Tobey was a seafaring man and knew his knots, so he "warmed a new rope, made a horse-knot, and put it round the horse's neck in proper style." He then went to the horse's stall in the barn and fashioned a brace, making escape virtually impossible. Finishing the job, he went into the Daggett's house to visit for a short while, and then left for home, but not before a final check of the horse in the barn.

To his surprise, the horse and the rope were gone. By this time, it was dark, so Captain Tobey returned to the house, fetched Samuel and a lantern, and went to search for the horse.

They found him standing in a "remote part of the barn." He was still wearing his collar, but had somehow broken free from the brace. Again, they tied him in his stall.

The horse kept getting loose. One time, he was found on the haymow with the rope "stuck so far into the hay it required two or three men to pull it out." Another time, "the waxed ends" (used about the seizing) "were found lying uncut where the animal had been standing." It seemed no one could determine *how* the horse was managing to escape his bonds. He would not move if he were being watched, only breaking free when no one was looking.

Then someone came up with a plan to tie the horse in his stall and nail the barn door shut for the night. Snow was brushed around the door, which would show the tracks if anyone tried to sneak in to free the animal. When morning came, the horse was loose, outside the barn, and the only tracks in the snow were the scrapes made by his shoe-clad hoofs when he'd crawled out from under the sill to get outside. From the size of the sill, it appeared to all present, to be an impossible feat.

They deduced it could only be witchcraft; surely, Daggett's horse was bewitched. This prospect excited the whole community, which turned out in droves to see the bewitched horse escape Daggett's barn at dusk. People came from as far away as Searsmont, and on some nights their numbers were as high as 150.

Someone must have persuaded Samuel Daggett to put an end to all this, for bewitchery and witchcraft was considered a form of devilry; thus, "the tips of the horse's ears were cut off and to the bleeding ends was applied a red-hot shovel."

Apparently, this ended the whole affair and the bewitching ceased.

Elizabeth Smith

On November 17, 1796, *The Eastern Herald and Gazette of Maine* contained an article titled, "Witchcraft." It described the court case, the previous week, of the Commonwealth against Elizabeth Smith [et al].

She was a widow in Biddeford, Maine, who apparently had to seek shelter in another town for her own safety, after her neighbor, John Hilton, went insane and accused her of bewitching him. According to Hilton, he had been on his way home around dusk in October, when the ox goad (cattle prodding stick) he'd been carrying was very nearly drawn out from his grasp by means of witchcraft. When he tried to strike Elizabeth Smith, whom he deemed was the source, he "received a violent blow" to his lower back.

He then went to her house in order to "obtain some of her blood." This resulted in a vicious assault upon Elizabeth Smith: he beat her with a stick, drove her outside, and then proceeded to choke her.

Judge Wells informed the court that the problems in this neighborhood "arose rather from ignorance in themselves than from witchcraft in the poor old woman." He then ordered them to keep the peace.

Old Nabbie

Old Nabbie lived near the "Witch Trot" road at Wells, Maine, in a little, run-down black house "untidily kept." Her familiar was said to be a black hog that entered and exited the door of her home at will. She also kept a black cat, and aside from these companions, lived alone.

A story is told of how one of Nabbie's neighbors was churning cream for butter one winter day and when, after a long while of churning and the cream hadn't turned, she suspected "Nabbie was inside the churn, bewitching the butter." Frustrated, the young woman poured the contents of her churn into the fire. She had expected to find some sign of Nabbie's doing there, but there was none to be seen, so she put on her shawl and headed for Nabbie's house to confront the woman.

Arriving at Nabbie's home, she asked to borrow some butter, assuming that if Nabbie *had* butter on hand, the old woman had certainly stolen it from her churn.

Old Nabbie informed her she fell into the fire that day and was so badly burned she would likely die from her injuries. Dressed in red flannel, she smelled strongly of brimstone. When Nabbie's black cat drew back and hissed at the guest, she fled out the door in fear.

Nabbie lived out her days in Wells, died "a peaceful death" and was given a proper Christian burial.

"Aunt" Woodward

In the early 1800s, "Aunt" Woodward lived by herself in a little log cabin in Minot Corner, Maine. She was believed to be a witch. Some of her neighbors kept her away from their house by nailing horseshoes over the doors, while others placed branches of "round wood" at their thresholds. They believed she "laid charms" upon their provisions and utensils, for example: souring fresh milk, spoiling eggs, and making items go missing. Children were particularly frightened of her; one girl avoided her lest she be "changed, between two days, into a white horse." When According to the legend, shortly before her death, her neighbor Mr. Blaisdell offered Aunt Woodward a ride. After she climbed aboard his wagon, his four oxen couldn't budge an inch, yet when she got out, they pulled the wagon *plus* a load of wood without effort.

Connecticut

Alice Young

Alice Young of Windsor, Connecticut, was the first person executed for witchcraft in America. She was hung from the gallows at Meeting House Square (where the Old State House is today) in Hartford on May 26, 1647. She had been accused of stealing in 1646, but confessed to other crimes as well. All we know of her comes from two lines. One was in an entry dated May 26, 1647 in town clerk Mathew Grant's journal: "Alse Young was hanged." The other is from Governor John Winthrop of the Massachusetts Bay Colony: "One... of Windsor arraigned and executed at Hartford for a witch."

Alice's name is sometimes spelled "Alse" or "Achsah." She was probably born around 1600, the wife of John Young. Their daughter, Alice (Young) Beamon was accused of witchcraft in Springfield, Massachusetts in 1677.

Lydia Gilbert

Lydia Gilbert of Windsor was sentenced to death for witchcraft on November 28, 1654, after being found guilty of murdering Henry Stiles on October 3, 1651.

Lydia was the wife of Thomas Gilbert, and they lived with Henry Stiles, an older man, that they cared for. On November 3, 1651, neighbor Thomas Allyn's musket accidentally discharged, killing Henry. Thomas pled guilty to "homicide by misadventure," and was fined £20 for "sinful neglect and careless carriages in the premises." For good behavior for one year, in which he would bear no arms, Thomas paid a bond of £10.

Lydia Gilbert, however, paid with her life. We are not given any of the reasons why she was suspected, only that six of the jurors in her trial were residents of Windsor, and well aware that Thomas Allyn had confessed and been convicted of killing Stiles three years earlier. Despite this, she was indicted:

> "Lydea Gilburt thou are here indited by that name of Lydea Gilburt that not having the feare of god before thy Eyes thou hast of late years or still dust give Entertainment of Sathan the great Enemy of god and mankind and by his helpe hast killed the Body of Henry Styles besides other witchcrafts for which according to the law of god and the Established Law of the commonwealth thou Deservest to Dye."

Research by J. Wingate Thornton states Jonathan Gilbert was Marshall of the Colony at the time of Lydia's trial. How horrible it must have been for him to have to condemn his own mother to death!

Some sources say Lydia escaped execution, however most historians believe she was hung in

Hartford on or around November 28, 1654. No documents exist of her execution/death. After her trial, Thomas Gilbert left Windsor and relocated in Nayang, Connecticut.

Mary Johnson

In 1646, Mary Johnson of Wethersfield, Connecticut, was sentenced to be whipped for theft, likely at Hartford, repeated a month later at Wethersfield. On December 7, 1648, a jury for "familiarity with the Deuill" [sic] indicted her. She confessed witchcraft in that she had gotten the Devil to fetch some hogs. She admitted to murdering a child as well as committing "faults of licentiousness." Several months before her execution, she gave birth to a son while in prison. Her jailer, William Ruscoe, agreed to raise and educate the boy.

John and Joan Carrington

John and Joan Carringtons of Wethersfield were executed for witchcraft in 1651. John was a carpenter who immigrated to America and settled in Wethersfield before 1643. Joan was his second wife. They were indicted on February 20, 1651. Governor John Haynes was present with magistrates. Both were found guilty on March 6, 1651.

Katharine Harrison

A Hartford jury found Katharine Harrison of Wethersfield guilty of witchcraft in October 1669, but the court did not approve the verdict and dismissed the case. She was, however, banished from the colony.

Mary "Goody" Bassett

Mary "Goody" Bassett of Stratford, Connecticut, was the wife of cobbler and town drummer, Robert Bassett. A mother of at least three children, she confessed to her crimes in a trial attended by Governor Haynes. After Mary's execution in May 1651 (likely at Fairfield, although tradition says "Witches Rock," at the crossroads of present-day Linden Avenue and Broad Street), Robert moved to Hempstead, Long Island, New York, and died there in 1670.

Goodwife Knapp

In early 1654, Goodwife Knapp of Fairfield, Connecticut, was hung at the gallows in Try's Field in Fairfield for the crime of witchcraft. She was probably tried at Hartford. She may have been Elizabeth, the wife of Roger Knapp.

On the day of her condemnation, a committee visited Goodwife Knapp in her jail cell consisting of: Mrs. Sherwood, Mrs. Odell, Mrs. Pell and her two daughters, Mrs. Lockwood, and Mrs. Purdy. They urged her to name other witches in Fairfield.

Poor Goody Knapp maintained her innocence; she just wanted to be left alone. "I must not render evil for evil...I have sins enough all ready, and I will not add this to my condemnation." She pled with them, "Never, never [a] poor creature was tempted as I am tempted. Pray, pray for me." They would hound her even after death, searching her corpse for witch marks; the worst of the lot was ringleader, Goodwife Staples.

In sheer terror at her impending death, Goodwife Knapp came down from the ladder and asked to speak to Roger Ludlow alone. She told him, no doubt hoping to buy her a little more time on this earth, that Goodwife Staples was a witch.

This confession was noted, and Knapp's execution commenced.

After Goodwife Knapp was executed, Thomas Staples attempted to clear his wife of suspicions of witchcraft in a series of trials whereupon he sued Roger Ludlow. This did not, however, result in clearing her character. In 1692, she was indicted on charges of witchcraft, tried, and acquitted.

Mercy (Knapp) Disborough

Mercy (Knapp) Disborough was thought to be the daughter of Peter and Sarah (Knapp) Disborough, and probably some relation to Goodwife Knapp. Mercy was the wife of Thomas Disborough, of Fairfield, and was tried with "two or three other women" at Fairfield for the crime of witchcraft. One of the other women tried at this time may have been **Elizabeth Clawson**. All were acquitted except Mercy Disborough. She was found guilty and sentenced to death, but it appears she was not executed. (Mercy and Elizabeth had been bound and "put into the water," where they "swam like a cork.")

Goody Ayres

Elizabeth Kelly was the 8-year-old daughter of John and Bethia (Wakeman) Kelly of Hartford, Connecticut. On March 23rd, 1662, she went to the home of Elizabeth Wakeman Willette, her maternal grandmother, and from there she went to the meetinghouse for 9 a.m. service.

At noon, she returned home, in the company of a woman of "checkered" reputation, Goody Ayres. Immediately upon entering the house, Ayres hurried over to the hearth where meat simmered in a pot over the fire. With a ladle, she drew some of the broth, and drank, then offered some to Elizabeth. Despite her parents' warnings that it was too hot, Elizabeth took some anyway.

She then complained of a stomach ache, and her father gave her a bit of powdered angelica root to ease the pain. It seemed to work, for two hours later, Elizabeth and Goody walked back to church for the afternoon service at 2 p.m.

That night, the Kellys were awakened by Elizabeth's cries. She had only been asleep three hours or so, when she'd woken up in severe pain and delirium. She claimed Goody Ayres was killing her. The Kellys tried to soothe their child, but there was nothing neither they nor anyone else could do. They believed their child had been bewitched to death.

Elizabeth Kelly died around midnight on March 26th.

Hers was to be the first autopsy performed in Connecticut, and this was the first death in America allegedly by witchcraft. Dr. Bray Rossiter of Guilford conducted the autopsy on March 31st. He found several suspicious symptoms, but as R. G. Tomlinson notes in *Witchcraft Trials of Connecticut*, these were "typical for a body dead that length of time."

In that day and age, it was sufficient "sound" evidence to warrant an arrest for Goody Ayres.

The trial began on May 13th. During proceedings, Goody stated that, "This will take away my life." Nathaniel Greensmith filed suit against William Ayres for slandering Rebecca, his wife. (It was a strange accusation: these people had been friends, and had shared "a night of merrymaking, under a tree on the green near Rebecca Greensmith's house. James Walkley, Goodwife Ayres and Goody Seager were present. They all danced and had a bottle of sack. Other nocturnal gatherings were held...")

A conviction for Goody Ayres was never reached; as soon as they got their first chance, William and Goody fled Connecticut. No one knew where they went, not even their 8-year-old son, John, whom they left behind. Their land and house, everything they owned, was taken by the colony. John went to live with the Ensign family and worked under James Ensign as a cooper's apprentice. He never saw his parents again.

One of their friends escaped at or around the same time: James Walkley ended up in Rhode Island.

Andrew and Mary Sandford

Andrew Sandford was indicted for witchcraft on June 6th, but the jury dropped charges. His wife, Mary, age 39, was indicted on charges of witchcraft on June 13th, and found guilty. She was hung at the gallows in Hartford, leaving behind her husband and five children.

Ann Cole

In 1662, Ann Cole of Hartford, Connecticut, daughter of John Cole, and neighbor of Nathaniel and Rebecca Greensmith, had been acting rather bizarrely and expressing apprehension about her "spiritual state." This was accompanied with "strange fits" of non-stop talking "for a considerable time." Most odd, was that some of time, Ann sometimes spoke in fluent Dutcha language she apparently did not know. To hear her imitate such exact pronunciations was both "very awful and amazing" for all who heard it.

She was also given to "extremely violent body motions…even to the hazard of her life." This often happened during church services, and sometimes accompanied by two other women "who also had strange fits." A special day of prayer was held for these ladies, but the noise and violence of their afflictions were of such magnitude that "a godly person fainted." Ann wasn't considered a witch, rather, she was bewitched.

On a day of fasting and prayer, Ann cried out that Elizabeth Seager was a witch. Upon hearing this, Elizabeth remarked, "Hodgepodge!" But Ann Cole was taken seriously and Elizabeth Seager was indicted.

After January 25, 1663, when Hartford had been cleared of its witches, Ann Cole's health returned to her at last. She "joined the church," married Andrew Benton, and had children. She led a pious life and died in 1686.

Elizabeth Seager

Elizabeth Seager was indicted for witchcraft on January 6, 1663, the same day as **Mary Barnes** of Farmington, Connecticut. On July 16, 1665, she was convicted, but the Court of Assistants found a cause to release her, after a year's imprisonment. She relocated to Rhode Island. It is not known what became of Mary Barnes, but according to records, a second woman was hung from the gallows for witchcraft on the same day as Nathaniel and Rebecca Greensmith; that unfortunate woman may have been Mary Barnes.

Nathaniel and Rebecca Greensmith

In court, Rebecca confessed that the devil first appeared to her in the form of a fawn, and little by little, would talk to her. They would meet near her house and he would come to her in the shape of a bird or animal. She also admitted giving him "frequent use" of her body.

She also testified about meeting under the tree in the green by her home with Mary James Walkley, Goody Ayres, Elizabeth Seager and others. They had a bottle of sack and they danced in the night. "Something like a cat" had called her out to this meeting.

Nathaniel, on the other hand, gave no confession.

The following indictment was read in the court held at Hartford on December 30, 1662:

> "Nathaniel Greensmith, thou art here indicted by the name of Nathaniel Greensmith for not having the feare of God before thine eyes; thou hast entertained familiarity with Satan, the grand Enemy of God and Mankind, and by his help has acted things in a preter naturall way beyond human abilities in a naturall course, for which according to ye Law of God and ye established laws of this Commonwealth thou deserveth to die."
>
> "The said Rebecca confesseth in open court, that she is guilty of the charge laid in against her."

Nathaniel and Rebecca Greensmith were executed by hanging at the gallows on January 25, 1663 for the crimes of witchcraft.

Hannah "Cranna" Hovey

Trumbull, Connecticut
Hannah Cranna Hovey had a few final requests. Who knows what might have happened if her wishes were fulfilled?

When Revolutionary War veteran Captain Joseph Hovey of Monroe, Connecticut disappeared, suspicions were quickly raised about town that his wife, Hannah, had something to do with it. (Some sources call her Hannah "Cranna" Hovey, but the Monroe Historical Society suggests "Cranna" was a nickname.) Searchers located Captain Hovey's body beneath a cliff, and while it appeared to be an accident, there was lingering doubt as to the *true* cause of his death.

Hannah had a reputation for cursing those who crossed her. Had Captain Joseph said or done something to set her off? It didn't take much; anyone who knew her also knew better than to risk her wrath. It wasn't so much that she had a bad temper. She did, but that wasn't the problem. The trouble lie with her words, her *predictions*. They had a tendency to come true.

On the other hand, her words could do powerfully good things as well. It was said that for those who expressed sufficient faith, she could make crops grow in rocky soil, or make rain appear or put a blessing on one's livestock or marriage.

Hannah had a large Shanghai rooster she called "Old Boreas," who used to crow at midnight with such precise accuracy, they could "set their clocks by his call." People used to claim clocks and pocket watches set by his call kept perfect time. Shortly after Old Boreas died, Hannah declared that her own death was imminent. "The spirits have called, and it won't be long before I'm in the Great Beyond." The month was January, the year was 1859, and she was 76 years old. She gave specific directions on how she wanted to be buried:

Her coffin had to be hand carried to the graveyard, and she must not be buried until after sunset.

When they found her dead in her dooryard the next morning, everyone wanted to fulfill her final wishes, but a snowstorm prevented hand-carrying Hannah's coffin to the crypt in the cemetery. Contrary to her instructions, they put her on a sled, drawn by horses, and as it made its way up the graveyard hill, the coffin fell off and slid back toward town. (Some say it came to a rest at the doorstep of her own house.)

The men reloaded Hannah's coffin onto the sled, secured it with chains, and started out once more. As the sled began to crest the hill, the sled and coffin began to shake under the strain of the weight. The horses pulled to a stop and Hannah's coffin was carried by hand the rest of the way.

By this time, the sun had set and the first stars of evening were beginning to twinkle. Her coffin was put in the crypt to wait for the spring thaw, when she would be buried beside her husband.

Upon returning to town, they found the Hovey house burning. No one dared go near it, "and it smoldered for weeks." Of course, everyone wondered if they had done exactly as she wanted in the first place, perhaps her house would still be standing. But who's to say? Sometimes the truth is stranger than fiction. To this day, "moans and strange occurrences" still happen on Cragley Hill (between Cutler's Farm Road and Elm Street) where she used to live. According to local historian, Ed Coffey, the rock where she used to sit can still be found on Cutler's Farm Road.

Hanna Hovey's gravestone can be found in the Gregory's Four Corners Burying Ground, located on Spring Hill Road in Trumbull.

New Hampshire

Rachel (Brasbridge) Fuller and Isabella Towle

In 1680, Rachel Fuller and Isabella Towle of Hampton, New Hampshire, were accused of witchcraft. It began in July when Moses Godfrey, infant son of John and Mary (Cox) Godfrey, became ill. His mother was holding him in her lap by the hearth and her 16-year-old daughter, Sarah, was present, when Rachel Fuller entered their home through the back door, as was her habit.

Her appearance startled them, for some brown, viscous fluid dripped from her face. It took the Godfrey women a few moments to realize it was molasses, but what was more shocking was it appeared she had bathed her face in it. It was daubed on so thick "that one eye was nearly covered and it almost dripped from her face."

Rachel sat down next to Mary and took Moses' hand in her own. Mary didn't know what to make of this, and snatched the boy's hand back, wrapping it in her apron.

Rachel turned from her, slapped the backs of her hands several times and spat into the fire. She then strew some herbs on the hearth and again sat down, saying, "This will be the worst day with it. Tomorrow the child will be well."

With that, she went outside, beat her arms as if they were cold three times, picked something up from the ground, and went on her way. The next day, Sarah and Mehitable told their mother that Rachel told them that if they laid sweet bays beneath the threshold, it would prevent a witch from entering the house. So the girls laid sweet bays beneath the threshold, all the way across the back door and half way across the front door.

It was not long before Rachel Fuller came to the front door. This was odd; she'd always come in before through the back door, which was next to her house. But the way she entered was odder still: crowding in against the side where the sweet bays had not been laid. She rubbed her back so hard against the post that it knocked off her hat. She came in, sat down, "and made ugly faces and nestled about..." She wanted to look in on sickly Moses, but Mary would not allow it. After this, she left the way she had come, but only after looking under the door where the sweet bays lay. This was the last time she entered the Godfrey home.

Little Moses Godfrey died a short time later. The Godfreys suspected witchcraft.

In July, Rachel (Brasbridge) Fuller, a mother of six or more, was arrested under suspicion of causing the child's death.

In court, Mary Godfrey and Elizabeth Denham testified that Rachel named several people in Hampton that she "reckoned for witches and wizards." Among those named were: Isabella Towle, Eunice "Goody" Cole, Benjamin Evan's wife and daughters, Grace (Swaine) Coulter and her daughter, Prescott, and one now dead. Elizabeth said Rachel told her witches did go out at night while their husbands and children were asleep.

Hazen Leavit testified about seeing Rachel on her hands and knees, scrambling about in her yard. Then he saw a "Thing like a little dog which came from the gate leading to her house." This "thing" went to her, while she was still scrambling about, putting things in her apron.

Nathan Smith said he was on his way home with his herd and was walking past the Fuller house when Rachel asked him if he'd heard the news in town. Smith said he didn't know of anything. She told him there was "a great row at Goodman Roby's." Evidently, it had been enough to get Dr. Reed up out of bed, "and with an enchanted bridle did intend to lead a jaunt, and he got her by the coat, but could not hold her." Nathan asked Rachel whom she was talking about, but she turned from him and he thought he heard her laugh.

On September 7, 1680, the Court decided that in the case of Rachel Fuller and Isabella Towle, that each owed bonds of £100. John Fuller became bondsman for Rachel, his wife. John Redman and Isaac Marston paid Isabella's bond. Isabella was in her late 40s at the time, a mother of nine. Her husband, Philip, was a seaman turned yeoman, and beyond this, not much more is known of her. Both women were discharged at the Dover Court on June 7th, 1681.

Eunice Goody Cole

> Goody Cole looked out from her door:
> The Isles of Shoals were drowned and gone,
> Scarcely she saw the Head of the Boar
> Toss the foam from tusks of stone.
> She clasped her hands with a grip of pain,
> The tear on her cheek was not of rain:
> "They are lost," she muttered, "boat and crew!
> Lord, forgive me! My words were true!"
>
> (From *The Wreck of Rivermouth* by John Greenleaf Whittier, 1894)

It mattered little that Hampton, New Hampshire's most familiar witch was wasting away in the Boston prison in the autumn of 1657 when the wreck of the *Rivermouth* occurred. So great and terrible was her reputation that Eunice "Goody" Cole became more famous in death than she ever could have been in life, given her circumstances. She became famous in 1938, when her life's story appeared in every newspaper across the country, and NBC dramatized it on the radio, and later that year on August 25th, her memorial service was broadcast nationwide.

Hers had been a most miserable, hard-scrabble life; in her later years, she'd been a social outcast, lived in abject poverty, tried several times for witchcraft, spent fifteen years in prison, died alone, and was even denied the dignity of a proper Christian burial.

In her younger years, she married a carpenter named William Cole in England. He was born about 1574. She and William worked as the indentured servants of Matthew Cradock, a wealthy London merchant. He furnished their passage to America for £10 when they were in their 60s; if they had any children, they were grown adults by this time. The Coles left them behind in England.

Their first home was in Massachusetts, then in Exeter, New Hampshire. By June 1640, William and Eunice were living in Hampton.

They were granted forty acres of land (upon which was an ancient well where mariners would stop to fill their water barrels, for it was believed this water would never go brackish). Despite this, the Coles were very poor. Eunice had a tendency to be loud and outspoken, and for this, she was taken to court many times between 1645 and 1656. The first charges included slander, illegal withholding of several pigs, and various other misdemeanors. In 1656, she was (likely) convicted of witchcraft and sentenced to a public whipping. The accusations against her had included causing the "strange death" of a calf (having poisoned its grass with a curse) along with a sheep, after town selectmen had refused her request for "wood and other things." She was accused of many crimes: of uttering curses that caused illness or death (like the deaths of three cows after having a quarrel with their owner); of keeping animal familiars, such as the grey cat she sent to sit upon and cause the death of ill persons, including an infant; of taking on various animal forms (shape shifting), and of having witch marks (mostly in the form of sores) upon her body; of causing strange, scraping noises to occur outside a house where two women were gossiping about her.

The Salisbury Constable's accusation was probably the most damning. Back then, there was no statue of limitations, and in almost every trial and inquest thereafter, it was brought up repeatedly. This man had been present when Eunice was stripped for her public whipping. Under one of her breasts, he saw "a blue thing like unto a teat hanging downward about three quarters of an inch long" and that, when some women were sent to examine it, "she pulled or scratched it off in a violent manner, . . . and she said it was a sore."

This blue teat was, according to the constable, the mark of a witch.

Later accusations would claim that she was suckling small familiars such as mice beneath her clothing.

Eunice spent the next several years languishing in the Boston jail. William used all of their meager savings to pay for her meals there. Finally, unable to tend the farm alone, the town of Hampton took possession of William's land. In a seventeenth century version of welfare, the town fathers used the proceeds to provide for the Coles for the remainder of their lives.

She was released from prison in 1660, but landed back in jail within a year or two. William died on May 26, 1662, at age 88. After his death, Eunice was released from jail, but was brought up on charges of witchcraft again. Serious accusations were brought against her: She was accused of enticing 9-year-old Ann Smith with plums and a baby if the girl would come live with her. When Ann refused, she claimed Eunice dragged her to an orchard and struck her on the head with a stone. After that, the old woman "turned into a little dog and run upon the tree," then flew off like an eagle. Ann added that Eunice appeared to her as a grey cat.

Anyone with half a heart would have understood why Eunice Cole wanted to take the girl into her home. Eunice was a lonely, old woman, and could have used even the help of a 9-year-old girl, but there is more to it than that. Ann Smith was a foster child. There were thirteen people in the family she was living with at the time of this trial "including 11 children with four different surnames." Ann's mother and adoptive father were dead. She had been uprooted from several homes already. Eunice must have seen an opportunity to provide the girl a stable home, perhaps not well off by any stretch of the imagination, but one she was willing to share. Her good intentions were spurned in the worst possible way, and Eunice was sent back to prison in 1673. She had been found innocent according to the indictment, but guilty of "familiarity with the devil." She was released, but not for long, returning to jail on September 7th, 1680, to be kept with a lock on her leg. The selectmen of Hampton were ordered to provide for her care while in prison. By the time of her final release, old woman was completely destitute, quite sick, and forced to live as a ward of the town of Hampton. A different family was required to bring her food and firewood every week. She only survived a few months.

When Eunice Cole died, she died alone; it was several days before her death was discovered. Her body was unceremoniously dragged out of her sorry little hut and pushed into a shallow grave. A stake was driven through her body to pin her to the ground, and from this, a horseshoe was hung to prevent her spirit from ever returning. Her age was estimated at around 88 years.

Today, no one knows the location of her grave, but it can be assumed, it was quite close to her home.

On Hampton's tercentennial in 1938, the people of Hampton voted to restore Eunice Cole to full citizenship and try to make amends for the wrongs done to her when she was alive. Certified copies of old documents containing her convictions were burned and the ashes were placed in an urn, along with some dirt from where her home used to be. The urn is in the Tuck Museum.

Tuck Museum

40 Park Avenue
Hampton, New Hampshire 03842-2159
Phone: (603) 929-0781
Web: www.hamptonhistoricalsociety.org/tuck.htm

The Tuck Museum is open 1-4 on Sundays, Wednesdays and Fridays. Admission is free.

In 1963, an unmarked stone was placed on the Tuck Museum lawn as a memorial to Mrs. Cole. Across the street in Founder's Park another stone reads: "Cole - 1640."

Goody Brown

The elderly widow Goody Brown was another accused witch from Hampton, New Hampshire, who lived during the 1700s on an isolated road. One day, a farmer stopped by to speak with her, and there must have been some trouble, for afterwards his pigs went missing. He blamed Goody Brown for their disappearance. This short description is the sole reference to the accusation of Brown's witchcraft.

General Jonathan Moulton

Aside from being a veteran war hero, having served in the American Revolution, a town official, a deputy to the colonial legislature, a land speculator and a shrewd businessman, "General" Jonathan Moulton of Hampton, New Hampshire, was believed by many to be in league with the Devil.

In March 1769, Moulton's mansion (house and property were estimated to be worth £3000) burned to the ground in a fire supposedly set by the Devil. According to the tale, the Devil was to be given Moulton's soul after so many times of filling a boot with silver and gold; this boot was hung in the chimney.

But the cunning general had cut the sole out of the boot, and the Devil did not notice this until he had filled the hearth with money, and for that, he set the house afire.

Before long, he had a new mansion built, even grander than the one before, with more rooms and better furnishings. When he died in 1788, the word of his passing spread "in no regretful tones." And when his body went missing just before burial, no one was really surprised.

It is said the Devil always comes back for his own. While this tale seems more fanciful than true, it may be purely proverbial: "Don't cut out your soul (or sole!) while waiting for the money to pour in."

Jonathan Moulton and ye Devil. *F. T. Merrill, 1906.*

Molly Bridget

Molly Bridget lived in the Portsmouth, New Hampshire, almshouse during the American Revolution, and there she was one of the more colorful characters. Everyone knew her as a fortune teller and a witch. In 1782, some pigs in the almshouse stye were declared bewitched; the only thing that could be done for them was to try the cure of snipping off the tips of their ears and tails. Then the snipped tips had to be burnt.

After the snipping, however, the snipped pieces of ears and tails could not be found. Clement March, the man who kept the almshouse, and who was in charge of procuring this remedy ordered "all the loose chips and leaves in the yard should be scraped up and burned in several fireplaces in the house."

When the fires started burning, Molly Bridget began racing from room to room "in a frenzied manner." Obviously upset, she then hurried to her own room and shut the door.

Whoever went to check in on her found her dead. A storm rose up at the hour of her funeral, for that was said to be another superstition marking a witch: to be buried during a storm.

"Granny" Hicks

After being denied a skein of yarn from a neighbor, Granny Hicks of New Hampton, New Hampshire, returned to her home. She was old and already under suspicion of witchcraft. When a woodchuck showed up on the neighbor's steps the next morning, and this was immediately followed by a child's death, most people in New Hampton had a hunch that it was the Granny Hicks' revenge for being denied the yarn.

Her neighbors believed she had turned into a woodchuck to lay a curse upon their family. In retribution, some of the townsmen took it upon themselves to wreck Granny's house with axes. Granny Hicks then told them how one of them would die, and although she never lived to witness their deaths, all of them died within a year exactly as she had predicted.

Massachusetts

Goody Morse

The jury found Goody Morse of Newbury, Massachusetts guilty at trial; however, Governor Bradstreet, Esq. and "some of the magistrates" reprieved her, unsatisfied with the Spectre Evidence used to convict her. On her deathbed, she declared her innocence of witchcraft, but confessed to her minister that she had "provoked the Lord by putting some contempt upon His word." This occurred while she was imprisoned for the crime of witchcraft, and had "suffered wrongly."

Mary (Reeve) Webster

Mary Reeve married William Webster in 1670. He was age 53, and she was a bit younger. They lived in Hadley, Massachusetts, were desperately poor and sometimes had to depend upon the town to get by. Mary had a bad temper, and her neighbors thought her a witch. She was often ill treated. In 1680, 16-year-old Ann Belding was charged with physical battery against Mary. Her father paid her fine: £1 to William Webster, £4 to the county.

It was said that ox carts or horse-drawn wagons nearing the Webster house were apt to become bewitched. Sometimes the animals would stop and begin running backwards. They would not even let the driver lead them past her home. Sometimes, a driver would enter the Webster house and threaten to whip Mary unless she allowed his team to pass. Occasionally, these men beat her.

Supposedly, she went to someone's home and caused an infant lying in a cradle to levitate so that it rose up off the floor three times "and no visible hand touched it." At another home, a hen fell down the chimney and was scalded in a cooking pot; at the same time, Mary appeared to suffer a scalding burn.

On March 27, 1683, she was indicted by the Northampton Court for "familiarity with the Devil," and sentenced to serve time at the Boston gaol. She was sent to Boston in April. On May 22nd, before the Court of Assistants with Governor Bradstreet, Deputy Governor Danforth and nine assistants present, Mary Webster was indicted for "not having the fear of God before her eyes, and being instigated by the Devil, hath entered into covenant and had familiarity with him in the shape of a warraneage [fisher] and had his imps sucking her, and teats or marks found on her, as in and by several testimonies may appear…"

Mary, approaching age 60, appeared before them again on September 4, 1683, to plead not guilty. After reading the indictment and evidences in the case, the jury found her not guilty.

Then Lieutenant Philip Smith became ill.

The following information comes from Cotton Mather who wrote of it in *Magnalia*. Smith was about 50 years old, a church deacon, a member of the General Court, a justice in the county Court, a selectman, and military man. According to Mather, Smith was concerned about Mary Webster's welfare, being that she was extremely poor, and of old age, and when he expressed this to her, her sharp tongue got the best of her. She evidently threatened him. He told Cotton Mather he worried about what harm she might cause him.

In early January 1685, he began feeling very fatigued, and suspected that Mary Webster had cast some sort of enchantment or spell upon him. He said to his brother who was caring for him, "...you shall see strange things. There shall be a wonder in Hadley! I shall not be dead when it is thought I am!"

In moments of delirium, likely beset with fever, he claimed Mary Webster was in his room. Some of Smith's friends went about disturbing Mary Webster, and while they were disturbing her, Smith was able to sleep comfortably.

Hutchinson provides the following information: Disturbing Mary Webster meant the "brisk lads" dragged Mary from her house, hung her up outside until she was nearly dead, took her down, rolled her in snow, then buried her in the snow and left her for dead.

Back to Cotton Mather's account. Strange events were witnessed in Smith's sickroom: unexplainable scratching noises about the bed, medicines "unaccountably emptied," fires on the bed that "vanished away," some unseen thing stirring on the bed, "as big as a cat," that no one could grasp, and mysterious bed shaking.

Lieutenant Philip Smith died on Tuesday, January 10, 1685. Bruises were found on his back along with "several holes that seemed made with awls." On Sunday, January 15th, "those who took him out of the bed found him still warm."

The next morning, however, his face discolored with black and blue. Fresh blood ran down one cheek. "Diverse noises" had been heard in the room where Smith's corpse lay, "but no account could be given."

Mary Webster managed to survive her ordeal in the snow. Some accounts claim she was sentenced for hanging in 1685, and she was left hanging from a tree all night. When she was cut down, she was still alive, and lived for over a decade. She did not, however, outlive her reputation.

Margaret Jones

Margaret Jones of Charlestown, Massachusetts, was executed as a witch at Boston on June 15, 1648. She'd been accused of the crime after an argument with neighbors, and a subsequent fire (barn fire?) to which she quickly attended out of concern.

She professed to her minister that she was wholly innocent of witchcraft, but admitted to the sin of stealing "something many years ago." She had long since repented for this, but must have wondered if this was some sort of divine retribution.

Alice "Goody" Lake

Alice Lake's maiden name may have been Pope. She was born about 1620, probably in England, and married Henry Lake. The Lakes settled in Dorchester, Massachusetts about 1640. They had the following children:

Elizabeth (Butts), b. abt. 1641, d. after 1702 prob. Little Compton, Rhode Island

Thomas, b. abt. 1642-3, d. 13 Dec 1715/17 Little Compton, Rhode Island

David, b. abt. 1644-5, d. aft. 1709, Little Compton, Rhode Island

Daniel, b. abt 1646-7, d. abt. 1652, Dorchester, Massachusetts

Infant, b. 1648-50

When Alice's baby died, she went out of her mind with grief, and told people her baby had returned to her. Because of this, the poor mother was accused of witchcraft. On the day of her execution, the court gave Alice an opportunity to recant the story about her baby returning, but she couldn't do that.

On the day of her execution, Reverend Thompson at Brantry visited her. While she "utterly denied her guilt of witchcraft," she also felt God was justified in bringing her to this punishment. She confessed that as a single woman she had "played the harlot" and finding herself with child, acquired an abortion. For this, she declared herself "a murderer in the sight of God for her endeavors," but for the crime of witchcraft, she was innocent.

Alice "Goody" Lake was hung at Dorchester in 1650.

Henry Lake immediately left Dorchester after Alice's execution, leaving their four surviving children as wards of the town. He relocated in Portsmouth, Rhode Island. Although the Lake children were raised in different households, twenty years later, they eventually reunited with their father.

Elizabeth "Goody" Kendall

When Robert Jenison's wife, Grace, gave birth to their second son, Samuel on December 15, 1642, he provided her with a local nursemaid for assistance. The Jenisons lived in Watertown, and when their baby died, their nursemaid (who claimed Goody had "bewitched the child to death") formally accused Goody Kendall of Cambridge of witchcraft.

Elizabeth "Goody" Kendall was born in England around 1600. She had come to Boston on the *Blessing* in 1635, as the wife of Samuel Holly. They moved to Newtown (Cambridge) and with their son, John, set up a mill. Samuel died in late 1643, and around 1644, Elizabeth married John Kendall of Cambridge.

Elizabeth Kendall was arrested but denied her guilt to the end. In late December 1642 or early 1643 (probably in Boston), she was executed for the crime of infanticide by witchcraft. On September 8, 1646, widower John Kendall sold the ten acres of land and the house his wife had inherited from Samuel Holly to Edward Jackson.

After the execution, Richard Brown, "knowing and hoping better things of Kendall," asked the Jenisons if they suspected Goody Kendall of bewitching their child. They said, "No."

The Jenisons believed their baby's death had been caused because the nursemaid had taken the child outside the night before he died, and it was very cold. Because she kept him outside so long, the baby became chilled. They said Goody had been by earlier that day, and "made much of their child," and they believed she would never do anything to harm him.

The nursemaid had killed their baby by keeping him outside too long in the cold.

After the accusing nursemaid (who was from Watertown), was imprisoned for adultery, and there delivered her child, Richard Brown went to her and told her it was "God's justice" to leave her to this wickedness as a punishment for her "murdering Goody Kendall by bearing false witness." The accusing nursemaid died shortly after while still in prison.

One of the most confusing factors of this case is that *both* the nursemaid and Elizabeth Kendall were nurses by profession, but Kendall worked as nurse for another family. The "nursemaid" hired by the Jenisons was a young, unmarried woman. Presumably, she committed adultery with a married man, subsequently became pregnant, and for that crime was sent to prison.

Mary and Winifred Holman

In 1659, John Gibson of Cambridge "had been troubled in the night with cats, or the Devil in their likeness, haunting of him." Apparently, so much so that he had to keep a light lit at night and a sword by his bed. One night he managed to strike one of the cats on the back, and after that his widowed neighbor, Winifred Holman had to see Dr. Day about a boil on her back. Gibson and his wife then entered a complaint of witchcraft against their neighbors Winifred Holman and her unmarried daughter, Mary. An arrest warrant was issued to the Constable of Cambridge on April 21, 1659, to bring the widow Holman and her daughter before the County Court in Charlestown for examination. An indictment was not reached, perhaps due to insufficient evidence.

Nine months later, on March 26, 1660, the Holmans sued the Gibsons for slander. At this trial, Mrs. Gibson gave testimony concerning her daughter's "fits" where she would cry out that Mrs. Holman and Mary were witches, "and that they must be found out, and said, you must not suffer a witch to live…" Mrs. Gibson said Satan had appeared at the bedside of this fitful daughter, and a while after (one of the court days), the daughter had gone into another fit, striking out at her family members, seeing and saying all manner of bizarre things.

John Gibson testified that in the winter of 1659 he could not keep the Holman's chickens out of his barn, and they destroyed the corn. He killed one with a stone and one of the Holman girls fetched it. After that, his own chickens, a brood of about fifteen, acted bewitched, "taken with fits." They would look upward and start twirling around, then run about as if mad. They subsequently died until there were only four left.

When the Gibson's spinning wheel would not work properly, they saw Mary Holman walking in a circle around an oak. When Mary left the oak, the spinning wheel worked perfectly.

In court, Winifred Holman presented the jury with two certificates signed by deacons and church members citing that in their opinion she had nothing to do with witchcraft. In the end, the Gibsons were fined and John Gibson was ordered to apologize for slander. The Holmans never appeared in court again on charges of witchcraft.

Ann Hibbins

Ann Hibbins was executed at Boston Common on June 19, 1656. Hers was an unordinary case in that Ann was the widow of William Hibbins, one of Boston's foremost men and leading merchants. He died two years prior to her execution, but during his life, he had served as deputy to the General Court, and was an Assistant from 1643 until he died. Ann herself was the sister of Governor Richard Bellingham (1641), who was serving as Deputy-Governor at the time of her execution.

Ann was first tried in 1655 and brought to trial before the General Court on May 14, 1656. The Governor in open Court pronounced her sentence: She was to go to the place of execution where she was to hang until dead.

> Hutchinson wrote: "…Search was made upon her body for teats, and in her chests and boxes for puppets [poppets], images, etc., but there is no record of anything of that sort being found…It fared with her as it did with Joan of Arc in France, some counted her a saint and some a witch, and some observed solemn marks of Providence set upon those who were very forward to condemn her."

She had three sons in England, and the youngest, Jonathan, set out for the colonies upon news of his mother's plight. She dated her will on May 27, 1656, stating that she wished for burial next to her late husband.

One of her contemporaries admitted Ann was hung "for a witch only for having more wit than her neighbors." Evidently, she had seen two of her persecutors on the street talking about her and this "cost her her life."

The Execution of Ann Hibbins. *F. T. Merrill, 1886.*

Ann was not destitute at the time of her arrest, but her husband had lost a great deal of money before his death. Hubbard states that £500 were lost due to the carelessness of a shipmaster and after that Ann "scarce ever was well settled in her mind...but grew very turbulent in her passion and discontented, on which occasion she was cast out of the church, and then charged to be a witch, giving too much occasion, by her strange carriage, to common people so to judge."

She died, according to Samuel Adams Drake, swinging from a bough of the Great Elm Tree, which stood in the center of Boston Commons, and unfortunately, she was not the last to die beneath its branches.

Mary (Lewis) Parsons

Hugh Parsons, a sawyer and mason, married Mary Lewis at Springfield, Massachusetts, on October 27, 1645. They had three children:

Hannah, b. 7 Aug 1646
Samuel, b. 8 Jun 1648, d. late Sep 1649
Joshua, b. 26 Oct 1650, d. 4 Mar 1651

In 1649, Mary was taken to court for slander of witchcraft against Widow Marshfield. She was found guilty and sentenced to receive twenty lashes or pay £3 damages. The Parsons opted to pay with twenty-four bushels of Indian corn. Shortly after this, their son, Samuel, died and Mary lost her mind. (This may have come about because of postpartum depression, or may have been a factor that led to it.)

In February 1651, Hugh and Mary were arraigned on formal charges of witchcraft. Mary was accused of "consulting with a familiar spirit and using diverse devilish practices" to injure Martha and Rebecca Moxon, two daughters of Reverend George Moxon. (There had been trouble between the two families over some brickwork Hugh had done on Reverend George's chimney; Hugh had been heard making a threat to "be even with him.") Hugh was likewise accused of injuring up to a dozen people. Mary pled not guilty and was cleared because of insufficient evidence. Hugh was in court under examination from February 27th to April 7th.

Much of the testimony was too fanciful to be taken seriously:

Hannah Lankton's boiled puddings were cut from end to end when she removed them from their bags, and who should show up at the door, but Hugh Parsons. Supposedly, "...the spirit that bewitched the pudding brought him thither."

Thomas Miller made some remark about Hannah Lankton's puddings to Hugh while they were eating dinner in the woods. When they returned to cut lumber, Thomas Miller cut his leg.

Blanch Bedortha suffered unusual pains after a quarrel with Hugh.

Even Mary relented that her husband had abused her and was often away from home.

Their son, Joshua, died on March 4th, and Mary, in a demonstration of insanity, declared herself a witch. She told how she lost a child (Samuel), and so longed to see him again...and the Devil appeared to her in the likeness of her dead child, coming to her bedside, and she received him into bed with her. This occurred several nights in a row, thus Mary "entered into covenant with Satan and became a witch." She also confessed to her infant's (Joshua's) murder. For this, Mary was sent to Boston for trial. Hugh joined her at the end of his examination. On May 13th, she was tried for witchcraft, but was found innocent. On the charge of murder, she was found guilty and was sentenced to die, but was reprieved until May 29th.

Mary was very ill in May, and since no record exists of her execution, it is very likely she died in prison.

On May 12, 1652, her husband, Hugh, was tried at a Court of Assistants in Boston for "having a familiar and wicked converse with the Devil," and of using witchcraft to injure "diverse persons." The jury found him guilty, but the General Court on May 27, 1652, determined he was innocent of witchcraft.

He left Springfield shortly thereafter and moved to Watertown where he remarried, and lived out his days.

Mary (Bliss) Parsons

Mary Bliss was born around 1628 in England and came to America with her parents when she was about eight years old. When she was around twelve, they moved to Hartford, Connecticut. In 1646, she married Joseph Parsons of Springfield, Massachusetts.

Joseph was a successful merchant; Mary was a successful homemaker. Together they had eleven children. Mary was a great beauty, but snobbish.

The Parsons moved to Northampton, Massachusetts, and not long after, in 1656, Joseph Parsons sued Sarah Bridgeman for slander of witchcraft against his wife, Mary. On October 7, 1656, the magistrates ordered Sarah Bridgeman to publicly acknowledge her wrongdoing, in both Northampton and Springfield, and failure to comply would result in a fine of £10.

Apparently, Sarah Bridgeman made her apologies, but after that, when anything wrong happened to the Bridgeman family, it was thought (at least by them) to be Mary Parson's fault. And of course, there was gossip about town concerning Mary and witchcraft as well.

In 1674, Mary Parsons found herself in court as a defendant. When Samuel Bartlett's 22-year-old wife, Mary (Bridgeman) Bartlett, died in July 1674, and it was suspected that she'd died an unnatural death, Mary Parsons of Northampton was accused of the crime.

Court proceedings began in Springfield on September 29, 1674, and finally concluded January 5, 1675. The court demanded a search of Mary's body for witch marks. The results were sent to Boston.

On March 2, 1675, Mary appeared at the Court of Assistants in Boston, then was formally indicted by the grand jury. She was ordered to Boston's prison to await further trial.

On May 13th, the Court of Assistants presented the indictments against her: "familiarity with the Devil" and "committing several acts of witchcraft."

She pled not guilty. The jury also found her innocent "and so she was discharged."

It wasn't really over, though.

When lumberman John Stebbins of Northampton died "in an unusual manner" on March 7, 1679, his body was later examined by Doctor Thomas Hastings of Hatfield in the presence of eleven Northampton men. The doctor found "several hundred spots, small ones as if they had been shot with small shot," upon his skin, along with some "other things not usual." Witchcraft was suspected. And of course, Samuel Bartlett, who happened to be John Stebbins' brother-in-law, jumped on this.

The Northampton court met on April 29, 1679, allowing Samuel Bartlett "to bring in such testimonies as he could find." The testimonies were sent to the Governor, but no one was prosecuted.

Ann "Goody" Glover

Ann "Goody" Glover was born in Ireland and spoke Gaelic, not English. She was Roman Catholic by faith, and a laundress by profession. In England, Oliver Cromwell had taken her and her husband during the occupation of Ireland in the 1650s. They were sold into slavedom in Barbados. After her husband was killed, she and her daughter made their way to the New World.

They settled in Boston's North End by 1680, and found employment doing laundry for the John Goodwin family. In 1685, a printed account of a recent witchcraft case in England involving bewitched children was circulating in Boston. Ann Glover never read it, but it is very possible a copy made its way to the Goodwin house.

In the autumn of 1688, 13-year-old Martha Goodwin noticed some linen was missing, and she assumed the family's laundress must have taken it. Martha went to the Glover's home and accused her daughter of stealing the linen.

Ann Glover gave the girl a piece of her mind in perfect Gaelic and sent her on her way. Of course, Martha had little to no idea of what Ann had *actually* said to her but there was little doubt the older woman was quite upset. How Martha made it home is anyone's guess, taking into account the condition she was in upon returning home:

Reverend John Cotton writes: "Immediately taken with odd fits, that carried in them something diabolical."

It wasn't long before this condition spread to the other Goodwin children. Eight-year-old Mercy, 15-year-old Nathaniel and 11-year-old John were "horribly taken with the like Fits."

How odd that at 9 or 10 p.m., the Goodwin children fell asleep and slept all night comfortably, but bright and early the next morning they were sometimes "deaf, sometimes dumb, and often all this at once." Their mouths would open wide, then their jaws would "clap together again, with a force like that of a spring lock." Their bodies would contort and they "would lie a benumbed condition."

The Goodwins deduced that Goody Glover had bewitched their children. In late September or very early October 1688, both Ann Glover and her daughter were accused and put into the Boston prison to await trial. While they were in prison, their home was searched for poppets and anything that might be used in the dark arts.

Ann's trial was particularly terrible because the poor woman didn't speak English, and she recited the Catholic (not the Puritan Protestant) version of the Lord's Prayer. The magistrates inquired of her sanity and appointed several physicians to examine her. They pronounced her sane; hence, she was found guilty and condemned. She told her accusers that killing her would not do any good.

At Boston Neck, about 11 a.m., on Friday, November 16, 1688, Ann "Goody" Glover was hung from the gallows. She was the last woman to be executed in Boston proper.

After her death, the Goodwin children's behavior became stranger still. Cotton Mather wrote, "...they barked at one another like dogs, then purred like so many cats." They would complain of the heat one moment and next shiver with cold. They'd yell as if struck, and "red streaks" would show up on their flesh. They'd fly "like geese," on the tips of their toes, arms flapping. One of them flew the length of the room in this manner, coming to land on a chair.

On November 16, 1988, Ann was exonerated from all charges of witchcraft and November 16th was proclaimed Goody Glover Day.

A plaque to commemorating Goody Glover as the first Catholic martyr of Massachusetts can be visited at:

Our Lady of Victories Eucharistic Shrine

27 Isabella Street
Boston, Massachusetts 02116

THE SALEM WITCH TRIALS

[The Salem witch trials have received so much coverage that most readers are already quite familiar with the sad account, and to take it into detail would require the length of another book. Hence, a condensed timeline of the events and people involved follows:]

1692

January 20th: Nine-year-old Betty Parris and her 11-year-old cousin, Abigail Williams, start having fits. Dr. William Griggs (probably) finds nothing physically wrong with the girls. Hindsight would tell him they are acting *exactly* like the Goodwin children of Boston four years earlier.

February: By this time, other girls in Salem begin to behave like Betty Parris and Abigail Williams. Baffled, doctors concur it must be the work of the Devil. The bewitched children interrupt services in the meetinghouse. In late February, they begin publicly accusing their neighbors of witchcraft.

February 29th: Sarah Good, Sarah Osborne, and the Arawak slave, Tituba, are arrested for witchcraft.

March 1st: Good, Osborne, and Tituba appear before the local magistrates for interrogation, then they are sent to jail. Tituba confesses to seeing a devil that appears "sometimes like a hog, and sometimes like a great dog." She claims there are *more* witches in Salem. It is likely she was physically beaten in order to extract a confession.

Tituba. *John W. Ehringer, 1902.*

More accusations follow: six-year-old Dorothy Good, Martha Corey, and Rebecca Nurse, all three of Salem Village, along with Rachel Clinton of Ipswich.

Magistrates John Hathorne and Jonathan Corwin examine Tituba, Sarah Good, and Sarah Osborne. Tituba confesses to the practice of witchcraft.

March 12th: Martha Corey is accused of witchcraft.

March 21st: Martha Corey is examined before Hathorne and Corwin.

March 24th: Rebecca Nurse is examined before Hathorne and Corwin.

Rebecca Nurse in Chains. *Freeland E. Carter, 1893.*

March 28th: Elizabeth Proctor is accused of witchcraft.

April 3rd: Sarah Cloyce, sister of Rebecca Nurse, is accused of witchcraft.

April 11th: Proctor and Cloyce are examined before Hathorne, Corwin, Deputy Governor Thomas Danforth, and Captain Samuel Sewall. During this examination, John Proctor is also accused and imprisoned. He had protested the examination of his wife, and becomes the first man accused of witchcraft in Salem.

Early April: Mary Warren admits lying about her neighbors and accuses the other "bewitched" girls of lying as well.

April 13th: Ann Putnam accuses Giles Corey of witchcraft.

April 19th: Abigail Hobbs, Bridget Bishop, Giles Corey, and Mary Warren are examined. Only Hobbs confesses. Mary Warren reverses her statement made in early April and rejoins the accusers.

April 22nd: Nehemiah Abbott, William and Deliverance Hobbs, Edward and Sarah Bishop, Mary Easty (another sister of Rebecca Nurse), Mary Black, Sarah Wildes, and Mary English are examined before Hathorne and Corwin. Only Nehemiah Abbott is cleared of charges.

She Stood Up Serene But Heroic. *Howard Pyle, 1907.*

April 30th: Several girls have accused Salem's former minister Reverend George Burroughs of witchcraft. His arrest warrant is issued.

May 2nd: Hathorne and Corwin examine Sarah Morey, Lydia Dustin, Susannah Martin, and Dorcas Hoar.

May 4th: Reverend George Burroughs is arrested at his home in Wells, in the Maine territory. During his extradition, a strange storm occurs.

Burroughs and the Sheriffs. *Alfred Rudolf Waud, 1878.*

May 7th: Reverend Burroughs is brought to Salem and put in jail.

May 9th: Hathorne, Corwin, Sewall, and William Stoughton examine Burroughs. One of the afflicted girls, Sarah Churchill, is also examined. Reverend Burroughs is moved to a Boston jail.

May 10th: George Jacobs, Sr. and his granddaughter, Margaret, are examined before Hathorne and Corwin. Margaret accuses her grandfather and Reverend Burroughs of witchcraft. Sarah Osborne dies in prison at Boston at age 49.

May 14th: Increase Mather arrives in Boston with a new charter and the new governor, Sir William Phipps, from the Maine territory. The charter ends the 1684 prohibition of self-governance within the American Colony.

May 18th: Released from jail, Mary Easty is re-arrested due to the outcries and protests of her accusers. Dr. Roger Toothaker is arrested on charges of witchcraft.

May 20th: Mary Easty is arrested once more, this time after being accused of bewitching Mercy Lewis with a sickness.

May 23rd: Susannah Sheldon accuses Philip English of murdering Joseph Rabson.

May 27th: Governor Phipps sets up a special Court of Oyer and Terminer comprised of seven judges to try the witchcraft cases. Appointed are Lieutenant Governor William Stoughton, Peter Sergeant, Nathaniel Saltonstall, Wait Still Winthrop, Bartholomew Gedney, Samuel Sewall, John Richards, Jonathan Corwin and Judge John Hathorne.

These magistrates base their judgments and evaluations on various kinds of evidence including:

1. Direct confessions
2. Supernatural attributes ("witch marks")
3. Reactions of the afflicted girls
4. Spectral evidence (the ability of a witch to leave her physical body and assume, if he/she wishes, another form; the Devil himself can also assume the "specter" of a witch)

May 31st: Hathorne, Corwin, and Gednew examine John Alden, Phillip English, Martha Carrier, Wilmott Redd, and Elizabeth Howe. Alden and English later escape prison and do not return to Salem until after the end of the witch trials.

June 1st: Mary, wife of Philip English, tells the court Mary Warren confessed to perjury.

June 2nd: Initial session of the Court of Oyer and Terminer: Bridget Bishop is first to be condemned to death.

Early June: Soon after Bridget Bishop's trial, a displeased Nathaniel Saltonstall resigns from the court.

June 8, 1692: Eighteen-year-old Elizabeth Booth shows symptoms of being bewitched.

June 10th: Bridget Bishop is hung at Gallows Hill in Salem, the first official execution of the Salem witch trials. Some people sign petitions on behalf of the accused people they believe to be innocent, hoping the petitions will end the trials.

June 15th: Cotton Mather writes a letter requesting the court not to use Spectral Evidence as a standard. He urges that the trials be speedy. The Court of Oyer and Terminer pays more attention to the request for speed and ignores his criticism of Spectral Evidence.

June 16th: Dr. Roger Toothaker dies in prison at age 58.

June 29th-30th: Sarah Good, Sarah Wildes, Rebecca Nurse, Susannah Martin, and Elizabeth Howe are tried and condemned to death.

Mid-July: Joseph Ballard of Andover enlists the aid of the accusing girls of Salem; thus begins the Andover witch hunt.

July 19th: Sarah Good gives birth in prison and the infant dies. She, Sarah Wildes, Rebecca Nurse, Susannah Martin, and Elizabeth Howe are executed at Gallows Hill.

August 5th: Reverend George Burroughs, George Jacobs, Sr., Martha Carrier, John and Elizabeth Proctor, and John Willard are tried and condemned to death.

August 19th: Reverend George Burroughs, George Jacobs, Sr., Martha Carrier, John Proctor, and John Willard are executed on Gallows Hill. The execution of pregnant Elizabeth Proctor is delayed.

August 20th: Margaret Jacobs recants her accusations that led to the executions of her grandfather George Jacobs, Sr. and the Reverend Burroughs.

September 9th: Martha Corey, Mary Easty, Alice Parker, Ann Pudeator, Dorcas Hoar, and Mary Bradbury are tried and condemned to death.

Martha Corey and Her Persecutors. *F. T. Merrill, 1883.*

Mid-September: Giles Cory is indicted on charges of witchcraft but refuses to testify.

September 17th: Ann Foster, Margaret Scott, Wilmott Redd, Samuel Wardwell, Mary Parker, Abigail Faulkner, Rebecca Eames, Mary Lacy, and Abigail Hobbs are tried and condemned to death.

September 19th: Sheriffs administer *Peine Forte Et Dure* (pressing of weights) to Giles Cory after he refuses to enter a plea to the charges of witchcraft against him. This took place in a field (now the Howard Street Cemetery), located next to the old Salem Jail. After two days of suffering under the weights, Cory dies.

September 21st: Dorcas Hoar is the first of those pleading innocent to confess. Because of this, her execution is delayed.

September 22nd: Martha Cory, Mary Parker, Margaret Scott, Mary Easty, Alice Parker, Ann Pudeator, Willmott Redd, and Samuel Wardwell are hung.

October 3rd: The Reverend Increase Mather, President of Harvard College and father to Cotton Mather, denounces the use of Spectral Evidence in court.

October 8th: After twenty people are executed in the Salem witch hunt, Thomas Brattle writes a letter criticizing the trials. This letter has great impact on Governor Phips, who then orders that reliance on Spectral and intangible evidence no longer be allowed in trials.

October 29th: Governor Phips officially dissolves the Court of Oyer and Terminer. He prohibits further arrests and releases many accused of witchcraft.

November 25th: The General Court of the colony creates the Superior Court to try the remaining witchcraft cases that took place in May of 1693. This time **no one is convicted** of witchcraft, and Spectral Evidence is no longer admissible in a court of law.

1693

January 3rd: Judge Stoughton orders the executions of all suspected witches who were exempted by their pregnancy. Gov. Phips vigorously denies enforcement of the order, and Stoughton angrily leaves the bench.

Tituba is released from jail. She is sold to a new master and leaves Salem.

May: Gov. Phips pardons all those still in prison on witchcraft charges. Of the surviving prisoners, forty-nine of the fifty-two are released because their arrests were based on Spectral Evidence.

1697

January 14th: The General Court orders a day of fasting and soul-searching for the tragedy at Salem. Samuel Sewall publicly confesses error and guilt.

Salem's Minister Samuel Parris is ousted and replaced by Minister Joseph Green.

1702

The General Court declares the 1692 witchcraft trials unlawful.

1706

Ann Putnam, one of the accusatory ringleaders, publicly apologizes for her actions fourteen years earlier.

1711

The colony passes a legislative bill restoring the rights and good names of some of those accused of witchcraft and pays 600 pounds in restitution to their heirs.

1757

June 16th: Salem Village is renamed Danvers and is incorporated as a town.

Massachusetts formally apologizes for the events of 1692. State legislature passes a resolution exonerating the accused and executed Ann Pudeator.

1992

August: On the 300th anniversary of the trials, Nobel Laureate Elie Wiesel dedicates The Witch Trials Memorial. Maggie Smith and James Cutler designed the Memorial. It consists of twenty granite benches built into a stonewall near the Old Burying Point. Each bench is inscribed with the name of the accused, the means and date of execution. Words of the victims are also engraved, many of them cut short, as a reminder of their innocence and the injustice done to them.

2001

October 31st: Massachusetts Acting Governor Jane Swift signs into law a bill officially exonerating Susannah Martin, Bridget Bishop, Alice Parker, Margaret Scott, and Wilmot Redd who were executed during the witch trials of 1692.

Salem, Massachusetts, was not alone in its strange and pitiful tales of bewitching. In nearby towns: Hogs were said to run about upon their hind legs; a man kept rolling across a floor and had to be watched so he wouldn't roll into the hearth; loaves of freshly-made bread were found full of hair; soap boiled over in kettles; stones fell down chimneys and broke dishes; strange fiddling was heard at night; flashing lights were seen and stones were thrown by unseen hands. Cape Ann and Gloucester were under guard against the "spectre leaguers," (devils attempting "a moral perversion of the colony").

Even after the madness of the Salem witch trials, the belief in witchcraft was still rampant throughout New England, as demonstrated by the following:

Goody Hallet

Goody Hallet of Wellfleet, Cape Cod, Massachusetts, was seduced at age 15 by the smooth-talking "gentleman" pirate, Sam Bellamy. She became pregnant and after the child was born, it died. She was charged with its murder.

While she awaited her trial in the jailhouse, she escaped…but that does not mean she was never seen again. Supposedly, in order to procure her escape, she entered into a pact with Satan.

In 1717, Bellamy's ship, the *Whiddah*, wrecked and his body floated to the shore not far from Goody Hallet's cottage.

Some claim that Goody Hallet's ghost is sometimes seen at night, dancing in a red dress upon the Wellfleet village green.

Moll Pitcher

Moll Pitcher, granddaughter of the benevolent wizard John Dimond, was a Lynn, Massachusetts, fortune teller famous for her ability to forewarn ship captains of mutinies and storms. According to the legend about her, she could get carried away; once, she badly frightened a girl who'd come to her for news of her man at sea, telling of his terrible death. The poor girl was mind-addled until her lover's ship returned and her senses were restored. Moll Pitcher died. In a strange twist of fate, the woman who prepared Moll's body for burial happened to be the daughter of the mariner whose death Moll mispredicted years earlier.

Abigail (Rogers) Dudley

In 1720, Abigail (Rogers) Dudley, the wife of Samuel Dudley, Esq. (son of Massachusetts Governor Francis C. Dudley) was accused of witchcraft by three neighborhood girls: Elizabeth Blanchett (age 11), and her sisters Joanna (age 9), and Mary (age 7). No formal charges were brought against Abigail, a pregnant mother of nine. Littleton minister, Reverend Shattuck, the minister of Littleton, Massachusetts, suggested that the Blanchetts separate their daughters. The Blanchetts refused and their daughters carried on with their "fits and "predicaments."

Abigail died shortly after giving birth to her tenth child, thus ending any claims made against her. The Blanchetts moved to Medford, Massachusetts, where in 1728, Elizabeth Blanchett confessed to Reverend Ebenezer Turell that she and her sisters made up the false accusations against Abigail Dudley.

Margaret "Old Meg" Wesson

According to the legend, the witch Margaret "Old Meg" Wesson of Cape Ann, Massachusetts, kept a raven as a familiar, and this bird had a crooked, white line beneath one wing. In 1745, Meg cursed Sir William Pepperell's soldiers at a local tavern just before they left on a march to the French fortress at Louisburg on Cape Breton.

At Louisburg, one of soldiers shot a bird that looked much like Old Meg's pet raven, breaking its leg. Another shot killed the bird. (According to the legend, they had to use silver bullets, for no other kind would harm it.) Upon returning to Cape Ann from their victory at Louisburg, a journey of about 500 miles, the soldiers were informed that Meg Wesson had suffered a broken leg the same day they had shot the raven. She died on June 16, 1745, just two days prior to the victory at Louisburg. (The legend also states that upon examination of her body, two silver bullets were extracted from Old Meg's flesh.)

Native American Witches

The Native American witch was one who performed taboo acts (such as murder or cannibalism) in exchange for forbidden powers. The shaman or medicine man was not a witch in that he *helped* the tribe and contributed to the good of the people. The witch, on the other hand, was considered a parasite, and, in some cases, a pseudo human.

Anthropologist Deward Walker, Jr. asserted the impossibility of defining a witch in universal terms, for each tribe had different practices and beliefs. Witchcraft persecutions did occur in Seneca, Chickasaw, Natchez, and Shawnee tribes as recorded by historians during the 1700s and 1800s.

In *The American Indian (Uh-nish-in-na-ba)* (1888), Elijah M. Haines tells of "about fifty persons, charged with being witches, were burned to death at the Onondaga castle. The witchcraft delusion prevailed among all the cantons. The last two persons executed for witchcraft among the Oneidas, it is said, were two females, about the year 1800, with the executioner being the notorious Hon Yost of Revolutionary memory, and the execution was done in accordance with the decree of the council, the mode being that of striking the victims with the tomahawk."

Most tribes believed in the witch's ability to shape-shift, for instance, into a fast-running animal or a bird that flew away. Witches were also believed to change themselves into inanimate objects such as a rock or log. They had intimate knowledge of natural poisons with which they used to harm their victims. Like the European settlers, they also believed in the witch's capability to bewitch others. Some thought they could blow worms or hairs into people's bodies. They caused sickness, accidents, death, and ill luck...and were capable of making the bravest man tremble.

The tribes took care of their witches themselves without any interference from white settlers. The tribal councils conducted their own trials in the accusation and condemnation of a witch "with great caution," writes Haines, "...lest the conjurer should get the advantage over them and thus bewitch the whole assembly."

Interestingly, prior to the European colonization, Native American witches were usually from *another* tribe, especially an enemy camp; but after white settlers arrived, witchcraft was usually discovered *within* the tribe. This change coincided with the colonial witchcraft persecutions. Walker asserts that contact between the settlers and the tribes increasingly interfered with what we would term "normal life" for the Native Americans. When faced with insurmountable changes in every aspect of their lives, it should come as no surprise that societies often turn inward for a possible solution. Their own kin sometimes accused tribal members of witchcraft after converting to Christianity. Later, relocation of tribes to reserved lands coincided with an increase of internal witch hunts. The Native American practice of killing suspected witches finally died out in the early 1900s.

Places to Visit in Salem

Salem, Massachusetts is the witch capital in the United States, and despite its carnival-like atmosphere, there are interesting places where visitors can learn what life was like back in the days of the witch hunts. Parking in the city is quite limited but most attractions are within easy walking distance. Trolleys and pedicabs are available during the warm months. Once you pay a ticket fee, it lasts all day, so visitors can get on and off the trolleys and pedicabs as often as they want.

The City View Trolley service makes nine stops throughout the city. As of 2009, trolley tickets were: Adults $12, $10 Seniors, $5 Children. Tickets can be purchased aboard the trolley, which stops include Essex, Central and Chestnut Streets, the Salem Common and Salem Ferry. Phone: (978) 594-0969.

Salem Trolley service also begins in April. This service makes 12 stops. Ticket prices as of 2009: Adults $12, Seniors $10, Children $3. Tickets may be purchased aboard the trolley. Stops include the Salem Witch Museum, Pickering Wharf and Chestnut Street.

Salem Pedicab are throughout the city and at the ferry terminal. Prices are $6 and up. Phone: (978) 835-3728. **The Witch City Rickshaw** are throughout the city and also at the ferry terminal. You pay only what you feel the ride was worth. Phone: (978) 979-9945.

Salem Witch Trials Tercentenary Memorial

Charter Street
Salem, Massachusetts 01970

An enduring memorial to the victims of the Salem Witch Trials, and a physical reminder to society to practice tolerance and understanding. Self guided. Open dawn to dusk. Free admission.

The Old Burying Point Cemetery

Charter Street
Salem, Massachusetts 01970

The oldest cemetery in Salem. Open from dawn to dusk. Free admission.

Death heads on gravestones were common in the Colonial era. This one can be seen on a head stone in Salem. *Sketch by Tom Gray, 2009.*

The Jonathan Corwin House (The Witch House)

Ira J. Patch, 1859
The Jonathan Corwin House

The only structure still standing with direct ties to the witch trials, the Jonathan Corwin House is believed to be the second oldest wood-frame house in the United States. Judge Jonathan Corwin lived in this home for 40 years. It has been open to the public since 1948.

310 ½ Essex Street
Salem, Massachusetts 01970
Phone: (978) 744-8815
Web: www.salemweb.com/witchhouse

Open daily May 1st - Early November, 10 a.m. - 5 p.m. Extended hours in October. Tours available off-season by calling.

Admission as of 2009: Guided house tour: Adults $10.25, Seniors $8.25, Children ages 7-14 $6.25; Self-guided tour: Adults $8.25, Seniors $6.25, Children ages 6-14 $4.25. Children under age 6 Free. Tour tickets sold at the museum gift shop.

House of the Seven Gables

House of Seven Gables. *Illustrated by T. M. Gray, 2009.*

This is the house made famous by Nathaniel Hawthorne. A guided tour of the Turner-Ingersoll Mansion (The House of the Seven Gables), Nathaniel Hawthorne House, the Counting House, Colonial Revival Gardens and waterfront.

115 Derby Street
Salem, Massachusetts 01970
Phone: (978) 744-0991
Web: www.7gables.org

Closed January 1 - 15 (2009). January 16 - June 30: 10 a.m. - 5 p.m. July 1 - November 1: 10 a.m. - 7 p.m. October weekends: 10 a.m. - 11 p.m. November 2 - December 30: 10 a.m. - 5 p.m.

Admission as of 2009: Adults $12, Seniors $11, Children 5-12 $7.25, AAA Members (with card) $11. Special events: Legacy of the Hanging Judge: $14, Spirits of the Gables $14. Group rates available by reservation; contact the Sales Manager at (978-744-0991 ext. 104).

Salem Wax Museum of Witches and Seafarers

The wax figures in this museum were fine-crafted in London and depict famous people from Salem's history. (There is a separate hands-on activity area for children.) The Old Burial Point cemetery is behind the wax museum and it is open to visitors. Candlelit Ghostly Walking Tours visit the Joshua Ward House, the Howard Street Cemetery, Old Salem Prison, and the Lyceum.

288 Derby Street
Salem, Massachusetts 01970
Phone: (978) 740-2929
Web: www.salemwaxmuseum.com

Tours available June, July, August and October, and may be booked at the website or by calling (978) 740-2323 ext. Tours must be booked in advance.

Open 7 days a week: January - March: 11 a.m. - 4 p.m., April - June: 10 a.m. - 6 p.m., July - August: 10 a.m. - 9 p.m., September: 10 a.m. - 6 p.m., October: extended hours, November - December: 10 a.m. - 5 p.m. Closed Thanksgiving Day, Christmas and New Years Day. For winter hours call: 1-800-298-2928.

Admission as of November - September 2009: Adults $7, Seniors and Students $6, Children $5. Children ages 5 and under Free. Hysteria Pass Admission: Adults $12, Seniors and Students $8, Children $11. Children ages 5 and under Free. Prices vary during the Halloween events. Discounts available for AAA members, Students and Military personnel with ID. Handicap accessible.

Salem Witch Museum

Salem Witch Museum. *Illustrated by T. M. Gray, 2009.*

A dramatic look at the witch trials of 1692, this is Salem's most visited museum.

19 ½ Washington Square North (Rte. 1A)
Salem, Massachusetts 01970
Phone: (978) 744-1692
Web: www.salemwitchmuseum.com

Open daily year round, 10 a.m. - 5 p.m. July - Aug. 10 a.m. - 7 p.m. Special hours in October. Closed Thanksgiving Day, Christmas and New Year's Day. Closes at 3 p.m. on Christmas Eve and New Year's Eve.

Admission as of 2009: Adults $8, Seniors $7, Children ages 6-14 $5.50. Group rates available.

Salem Witch Village

Salem Witch Village was created in conjunction with modern-day witches. Learn the truth of the legends, superstitions, and centuries of deadly propaganda concerning witchcraft…and find out what witchcraft really means. Tour a maze with a practicing witch. Special exhibits, workshops.

282 Derby Street
Salem, Massachusetts 01970
Phone: (978) 740-2929
Web: www.salemwitchvillage.net

Open year round, 7 days a week: April - June: 10 a.m. - 6 p.m., July - August: 10 a.m. - 9 p.m., September: 10 a.m. - 6 p.m., October: extended hours, November - December: 10 a.m. - 5 p.m., January - March: 11 a.m. - 4 p.m. Closed Thanksgiving Day, Christmas and New Years Day. Handicap accessible.

Admission: Adults $5.50, Seniors $5, Students and Children $3.50

Spellbound Museum

View authentic historical, cultural, and religious artifacts pertaining to the supernatural world. Items on display include a 200-year-old vampire-killing kit, various medical oddities, headhunter trophies, Voodoo altars, and much more. America's only "Ghost Gallery," and New England's only museum dedicated to the mysteries of the paranormal.

192 Essex Street
Salem, Massachusetts 01970
Phone: (978) 745-0138
Web: www.spellboundtours.com

Open daily (Spring - October 31) at 10 a.m. Call for November and Winter hours.

Admission as of 2009: Adults $10, Seniors and Students $7, Children under age 13: $5 (Admission prices to change in October).

Witch Dungeon Museum

Watch an acclaimed presentation of the trial of Sarah Good adapted from the 1692 historical manuscripts, performed by professional actors. Guided Dungeon tour recreates the atmosphere and conditions of the prison where the accused awaited their trials and executions. AAA approved.

16 Lynde Street
Salem, Massachusetts 01970
Phone: (978) 741-3570
Web: www.witchdungeon.com

Open 7 days a week. April - November: 10 a.m. - 5 p.m. Evenings during Haunted Happenings in October.

Admission as of 2009: Adults $8, Seniors $7, Children ages 4-13 $6.

Witch Dungeon Museum. *Illustrated by T. M. Gray, 2009.*

Witch History Museum

Watch a live presentation of authentic 1962 history and take a tour downstairs of the recreated Old Salem Village containing many life-size scenes.

197-201 Essex Street
Salem, Massachusetts 01970
Phone: (978) 741-7770
Web: www.witchhistorymuseum.com

Open daily April - November: 10 a.m. - 5 p.m. Groups welcome.

Admission as of 2009: Adults $8, Seniors $7, Children ages 4-13 $6.

Afterward

In Texas in 1915, a woman suspected of witchcraft was said to be stoned to death by her peers, despite rumors that she was a relative of a high-ranking public official. The last person to die in the United States because of witchcraft was killed in Pennsylvania in 1929.

There exists an interesting similarity between the actions of witches and alien abductions, and it's enough to warrant further study. Consider that the witch was believed to *fly through the air at night* and have sex with the devil. Many UFO abductees are taken at night, fly through the air, and are placed aboard a spaceship where "experiments" (sometimes sexual in nature) are conducted upon them. Were some of the witchcraft cases actually abductees?

Perhaps it's not so far fetched an idea. There are those today who truly believe aliens are actually demons or the fallen angels known as Nephilim.

Bibliography

Bard, Megan. "When Vampire Panic Struck Jewett City," *The Day*, New London, Connecticut: The Day Publishing Company, 27 Oct 2008.

Barber, John Warner. *Historical Collections of Connecticut*, Newark, New Jersey: Benjamin Olds, 1836.

Bassett, Wheeler A. *A Bassett Book*, Interlaken, New York: self-published, 1928.

Bell, Michael E. *Food for the Dead: On the Trail of New England's Vampires*, Carroll and Graf Publishers: New York, New York, September 2002.

Bethge, Philip. "The Healing Power of Death," *Spiegel International ONLINE*, Berlin, Germany, January 30, 2009, http://www.spiegel.de/international/zeitgeist/.

Birchfield, James D. *Thomas Satterwhite Noble 1835-1907,* Lexington, Kentucky: University of Kentucky Art Museum, 1988.

Bondeson, Jan. *Buried Alive: The Terrifying History of Our Most Primal Fear*, New York, New York: W. W. Norton and Co., 2002.

Booth, B. J., compiler, editor. *UFO Casebook*, Belton, Texas: www.ufocasebook.com.

Brainard, Homer W., Gilbert, Harold S., and Torrey, Clarence A. *The Gilbert Family: Descendants of Thomas Gilbert, 1582(?)-1659, of Mt. Wollaston (Braintree), Windsor, and Wethersfield*, New Haven, Connecticut: self-published, 1953.

Brewster, Charles W. "Witchcraft in Portsmouth," Brewster's Rambles About Portsmouth #144, *SeacoastNH.com*, Portsmouth, New Hampshire: Seacoast Media Group, a subsidiary of Ottaway Newspapers, Inc., (original, circa 1862), reprint 2000.

Bitten, Emma. *Nineteenth Century Miracles or Spirits and their Work in Every Country of the Earth*, Whitefish, Montana: Kessinger Publishing, 2003.

Boudillion, Daniel V. "Ceremonial Time: Fact or Fiction, Setting the Record Straight on the Dudley Witch Accusations of 1720 in Littleton," Littleton, Massachusetts: www.boudillion.com/witch/mitchell.htm, March 14, 2005.

Broad Brook Grange No. 151. *Official History of Guilford, Vermont 1678-1961 With Genealogies and Biographical Sketches*, Guilford, Vermont: Town of Guilford Vermont, 1961, reprint GHS, 1992.

Brooke, John Hendley. *Science and Religion: Some Historical Perspectives*, Cambridge, Massachusetts: Cambridge University Press, 1991.

Bryant, William Cullen and McMichael, George, ed. "Thanatopsis," (1817) *Anthology of American Literature*, New York, New York: Macmillan Publishing Company, 1985.

Burr, George Lincoln, LL.D., Litt.D. *Narratives of the Witchcraft Cases, 1648-1706*, New York, New York: Charles Scribner's Sons, 1914.

CAIPRS (Cape And Island Paranormal Research Society): www.caiprs.com.

Casey, Maura J. "Of Witches and the Wait for Justice," *The New York Times*, New York, New York: The New York Times Publishing Company, 13 Apr 2008.

Champoux, Art. "Incident at Exeter: a New Perspective," *UFODigest.com*, Port Colborne, Ontario, Canada: Dirk Vander Ploeg, publisher, August 7, 2007.

Citro, Joseph A. *Green Mountain Ghosts, Ghouls and Unsolved Mysteries*, New York, New York: Houghton Mifflin Company, 1994.

and Foulds, Diane E. *Curious New England, the Unconventional Traveler's Guide to Eccentric Destinations*, Hanover, New Hampshire: University Press of New England, 2004.

and Sceurman, Mark. *Weird New England*, New York, New York: Sterling Publishing Company, Inc., 2005.

Clark, George Larkin. *A History of Connecticut, Its People and Institutions*, New York, New York, G. P. Putnam's Sons: The Knickerbocker Press, 1914.

Clark, Jerome. *Unexplained!: 347 Strange Sightings, Incredible Occurrences, and Puzzling Physical Phenomena*, Detroit, Michigan: Invisible Ink, 1993.

The UFO Book: Encyclopedia of the Extraterrestrial, London, England: Visible Ink Press, 1997.

Colonial Society of Massachusetts. *Publications of the Colonial Society of Massachusetts*, Volume XX, 1917-1919, Boston, Massachusetts: Published by the Society, 1920.

Corliss, William R. "Archaeological Riddle," *Science Frontiers Online*, No. 67, Jan-Feb 1990, Glen Arm, Maryland: www.science-frontiers.com.

Strange Universe, Glen Arm, Maryland: The Sourcebook Project, 1975.

Craig, David V. "The Hampton Witch," *New Hampshire Echoes*, Hampton, New Hampshire: Lane Memorial Library, Jan/Feb 1973.

Crane, Elaine Forman. *Killed Strangely: The Death of Rebecca Cornell*, Ithaca, New York: Cornell University Press, 2002.

Cummings, Abraham, Reverend *Immortality Proved by Testimony of Sense*, Bath, Maine: J.C. Torrey, 1826 (New York Public Library).

Dana, Henry Swan. *History of Woodstock, Vermont*, New York, New York: Houghton, Mifflin and Co.,1889.

Davenport, Peter, director. National UFO Reporting Center (NUFORC), Harrington, Washington: www.nuforc.org.

Deloma, Jamie. "Vampires Haunted Settlers," *Worcester Telegram*, Worcester, Massachusetts: Worcester Telegram and Gazette Corp., November 25, 2007.

Demos, John Putnam. *Entertaining Satan - Witchcraft and the Culture of Early New England*, New York, New York: Oxford University Press, 1982.

Drake, Samuel Gardner. *Annals of Witchcraft in New England and Elsewhere in The United States, From Their First Settlement, Drawn Up from Unpublished and Other Well Authenticated Records of the Alleged Operations of Witches and Their Instigator, The Devil*, Boston, Massachusetts: W. Elliot Woodward, 1869.

Dunham, Christopher. "Witch Abusers Brought to Court," www.strangemaine.blogspot.com, Portland, Maine, 19 Apr 2006.

"Medical Cannibalism in Penobscot County," www.strangemaine.blogspot.com, Portland, Maine, 11 Nov 2005.

Durwin, Joe. "Bizarre Berkshires: Tales Spooky and Otherwise," *iBerkshires.com*, North Adams, Massachusetts: Boxcar Media, LLC, October 27, 2004.

Fawcett, Lawrence and Greenwood, Barry J. *Clear Intent*, Englewood Cliffs, New Jersey: Prentice Hall, Inc., 1984.

The UFO Cover-up: What the Government Won't Say, New York, New York: Fireside (Simon and Schuster), 1992.

Fowler, Raymond E. *The Allagash Abductions: Undeniable Evidence of Alien Intervention*, Columbus, North Carolina: Wild Flower Press (Granite Publishing, LLC), 1994.

The Andreasson Legacy, New York, New York: Marlow and Company, 1997.

Fuller, John Grant. *Interrupted Journey*, New York, New York: G. P. Putnam's Berkley Medallion Edition, Berkley Publishing Company, 1966.

Incident at Exeter, New York, New York: G. P. Putnam's Berkley Medallion Edition, Berkley Publishing Company, 1967.

Gauthier, Norm. *Norm Gauthier's Guide to New Hampshire "Haunted" Places You Can Visit!*, Hollis, New Hampshire: Puritan Press, 1988.

Gianninoto, Gordon J. "UFOs Sweep Across Maine," *Bangor Daily News*, Bangor, Maine: Richard J. Warren, publisher, January 30, 1998.

Gill-Austern, Maggie. "Odd Lights, Low Sounds Cause Stir," *Sun Journal*, Lewiston, Maine: James R. Costello, Sr., publisher, February 14, 2007.

Gray, T. M. *Ghosts of Maine*, Atglen, Pennsylvania: Schiffer Books, 2008.

Haines, Elijah M. *The American Indian (Uh-nish-in-na-ba)*, Chicago, Illinois: The MAS-SIN-NÁ-GAN Company, 1888.

Hall, David D. *Witch-Hunting in the Seventeenth-Century New England*, Boston, Massachusetts: Northeastern University Press, Second Edition, 1999.

Hale, John, Reverend. *Modest Inquiry into the Nature of Witchcraft*, Whitefish, Montana: Kessinger Publishing, 2003.

Hampton Historical Society: www.hamptomhistoricalsociety.org/

Hill, Frances. *A Delusion of Satan: The Full Story of the Salem Witchcraft trials*, Cambridge, Massachusetts: Da Capo Press, 2002.

Hoadly, Charles J., LL.D. "A Case of Witchcraft in Hartford," *The Connecticut Magazine*, Hartford, Connecticut: The Connecticut Magazine Company, November 1899.

Hobbs, Clarence W. *Lynn and Surroundings*, Lynn, Massachusetts: Lewis and Winship Publishers, 1886.

Hubbard, William, Reverend. *A General History of New England from the Discover to 1680*, Boston, Massachusetts: Charles C. Little and James Brown, 1848.

Huget, Jennifer. "Going to the Dog Chapel," *The Washington Post*, Washington, D.C.: The Washington Post Company, July 6, 2003.

Karlsen, Carol F. *The Devil in the Shape of a Woman: Witchcraft in Colonial New England*, New York, New York: W.W. Norton and Company, Inc. 1987.

Kimball, Henrietta D. *Witchcraft Illustrated to be Understood. Facts, Theories and Incidents with a Glance at Old and New Salem and its Historical Resources*, Boston, Massachusetts: Press of S. J. Parkhill and Company (George A. Kimball, Publisher), 1892.

Kittredge, George Lyman. *Witchcraft in Old and New England*, New York: Russell and Russell, 1929.

Lambert, Lane. "Dark Curses, Friendly Ghosts Abound on the South Shore," *The Patriot Ledger*, Quincy, Massachusetts: Gatehouse Media, Inc., October 27, 2008.

Lawhon, Loy. "The Hill Abduction," *UFO Evidence*: www.ufoevidence.org

Leech, Adam. "Looking to the Sky - UFO Reports Investigated," (article used with permission of Art Champoux), *UFODigest.com*, Port Colborne, Ontario, Canada, March 13, 2007.

LiBrizzi, Marcus. *Dark Waters, Chill Waters: Ghost Tales from Down East, Maine*, Camden, Maine: Down East Books, 2007.

Lore, Gordon I. R. and Denault, Harold H., Jr. *Mysteries of the Skies: UFOs in Perspective*, Englewood Cliffs, New Jersey: Prentice Hall, Inc., 1968.

Mansfield, David L. "History of Dummerston" by from *Vermont Historical Gazetteer*, Vol. 5, Burlington, Vermont: Carrie E. H. Page, 1891.

Mappen, M. *Witches and Historians*, Huntingdon, New York: Robert E. Krieger Publishing Company, 1980.

Marden, Kathleen and Friedman, Stanton. *Captured!: The Betty and Barney Hill UFO Experience: The True Story of the World's First Documented Alien Abduction*, Franklin Lakes, New Jersey: New Page Books, 2007.

Mather, Cotton. *Magnalia Christi Americana Volume II*, (1702), (reprint) New York, New York: Russell and Russell, 1967.

Mayo., L. S. *The History of the Colony and Province of Massachusetts Bay by Thomas Hutchinson*, Cambridge, Massachusetts: Harvard University Press, 1936.

Meurer, Terry Dunn and Cosgrove, John, executive producers. *Unsolved Mysteries: UFOs*, Los Angeles, California: First Look Home Entertainment, 2004.

Mills, Cynthia. "The Story of the Hubbard Memorial," *Vermont History*, 68, Barre, Vermont: The Vermont Historical Society, Winter/Spring 2000.

Nickell, Joe. "Entombed Alive!" *Skeptical Inquirer*, Vol. 32, Amherst, New York: Committee for Skeptical Inquiry, March/April 2008.

"Searching for Vampire Graves," *Skeptical* Inquirer, Vol. 37, Amherst, New York: Committee for Skeptical Inquiry, March/April 2009.

and Fischer, John F. *Secrets of the Supernatural: Investigating the World's Occult Mysteries*, Buffalo, New York: Prometheus Books, 1988.

Olson, Kris. "Does Fort Sewall Hold Spooky Secrets," *Wicked Local Marblehead (Marblehead Reporter)*, Marblehead, Massachusetts: Gatehouse Media New England, www.wickedlocal.com, August 21, 2008.

Paige, Lucius R. *History of Cambridge, Massachusetts, 1630-1877, With a Genealogical Register*, Boston, Massachusetts: H. O. Houghton and Company, 1877.

Pettibone, John S. "The Early History of Manchester," *Proceedings of the Vermont Historical Society*, Vol I, No. 4, Montpelier, Vermont: Vermont Historical Society, 1930.

Philips, David E. *Legendary Connecticut: Traditional Tales of the Nutmeg State*, Willimantic, Connecticut: Curbstone Press, 1992.

Poole, William F. and Windsor, Justin, editor. "Witchcraft in Boston," *The Memorial History of Boston*, Vol. II, Boston Massachusetts: James R. Osgood and Company, 1881.

Porter, Edwin H. *The Fall River Tragedy: A History of the Borden Murders*, Fall River, Massachusetts: J.D. Munroe, 1893, (reprint) Portland, Maine: King Philip Publications, 1985.

Radin, Edward. *Lizzie Borden: The Untold Story*, New York, New York: Simon and Schuster, 1961.

Revai, Cheri. *Haunted Connecticut*. Mechanicsburg, Pennsylvania: Stackpole Books, 2006.

Rhode Island Historical Cemeteries Transcription Project Index: www.rootweb.ancestry.com/`rigenweb/cemetery/cemetery004.html

Robinson, J. Dennis. "The Hex-ploitation of Goody Cole," *SeacoastNH.com*, Vol. 2, No. 14, Portsmouth, New Hampshire: Seacoast Media Group, a subsidiary of Ottaway Newspapers, Inc., October 24, 1998.

"Attack of the Rock-Throwing Devil," Vol. 7, *SeacoastNH.com*, No. 4, Portsmouth, New Hampshire: Seacoast Media Group, a subsidiary of Ottaway Newspapers, Inc., April 14, 2003.

"Real Vampires in New England?" *SeacoastNH.com*, Portsmouth, New Hampshire: Seacoast Media Group, a subsidiary of Ottaway Newspapers, Inc., 2001.

Salzman, Avi. "In 1647, the Capital Crime was Witchcraft," *The New York Times*, New York, New York: The New York Times Company, January 23, 2005.

Schenck, Elizabeth Hubbell. *The History of Fairfield, Fairfield County, Connecticut, From the Settlement of the Town in 1639 to 1818, Vol. I*, New York, New York: self-published, 1889.

Schevill, Ferdinand. *Karl Bitter, A Biography*, Chicago, Illinois: The University of Chicago Press, 1917.

Schlosser, S. E. *Spooky New England*, Guilford, Connecticut: Globe Pequot, 2003.

Sibley, John Langdon. *A History of the Town of Union, in the County of Lincoln, Maine, to the Middle of the Nineteenth Century with a Family Register of the Settlers before the Year 1800, and of their Descendants*, Boston, Massachusetts: Benjamin B. Mussey and Company, 1851.

Sifakis, Carl. *Official Guide to UFO Sightings: State by State Encounters*, New York, New York: Sterling Publishing Company, 1979.

Spinelli, Tony. "The Story of the Witch of Monroe," *The Connecticut Post*, Bridgeport, Connecticut: Hearst Corporation, October 29, 2007.

Steiger, Brad. "Taken!" *UFO Digest*, Port Colborne, Ontario, Canada: Dirk Vander Ploeg, 2008.

Story, Ronald D. *The Encyclopedia of Extraterrestrial Encounters*, New York, New York: NAL (New American Library), 2001.

Strange New England: http://strangene.com

Sullivan, Robert. *Goodbye Lizzie Borden*, New York, New York: Penguin Books, 1974.

Tannenbaum, Rebecca Jo. *The Healer's Calling: Women and Medicine in Early New England*, Ithaca, New York: Cornell University Press, 2002.

Tardiff, Olive. "Seacoast Women: Eunice Goody Cole (1590-1680) from They Paved The Way - A History Of NH Women," *Women for Women Weekly Press*, *SeacoastNH.com*, Portsmouth, New Hampshire: Seacoast Media Group, a subsidiary of Ottaway Newspapers, Inc., 1980.

Tarpinian, Gary, and Theeranuntawat, Paninee, executive producers. "Lizzie Borden Had an Axe," Burbank, California: MorningStar Entertainment (for the Discovery Channel), 2004.

Taylor, John M. *The Witchcraft Delusion in Colonial Connecticut, 1647-1697*, New York, New York: The Grafton Press, 1908.

Thomas, Keith. *Religion and the Decline of Magic*. New York: Charles Scribner's Sons, 1971.

Thompson, C. J. S. *Mystery and Art of the Apothecary*, (London, England: John Lane, 1929), Whitefish, Montana: Kessinger Publishing, 2007.

Tomlinson, R. G. *Witchcraft Trials of Connecticut*, Hartford, Connecticut: Bond Press, 1978.

Trask, William B., Whitmore, William H., and Dean, John Ward. "Witchcraft in Maine," *New England Historical and Genealogical Register Vol. XIII, No. 3*, Boston, Massachusetts: Samuel G. Drake, publisher, July 1859.

Trento, Salvatore M. *Field Guide to the Mysterious Places of Eastern North America*, New York, New York: Holt Paperbacks, 1997.

Tucker, James W. "The Witch of Hampton," *Hampton Tercentenary (1638-1938)*. Hampton, New Hampshire: Hampton Library, 1938.

Unknown. "Airship That Startled Farmers," *Massillon Independent*, Massillon, Ohio: Gatehouse Media, October 25, 2006.

Unknown. "EXHUMED THE BODIES - Testing a Horrible Superstition in the Town of Exeter - BODIES OF DEAD RELATIVES TAKEN FROM THEIR GRAVES," *Providence Journal*, Providence, Rhode Island: John Carter, publisher, March 19, 1892.

Unknown. "Sisters Estranged Over Nance O'Neill - Her Entertainment Causes Quarrel Between Lizzie and Emma Borden," *The San Francisco Call*, San Francisco, California: John D. Spreckles, Publisher, June 7, 1905.

Unknown. "Fighting Hard for a Life - Counsel in the Borden Murder Trial Begins Their Arguments - Earnest Plea of Lizzie's Lawyer - Ex-Governor Robinson Holds the Attention of the Jury - His Explanation of the Various Circumstances Connected with the Case," *The Omaha Daily*, Omaha, Nebraska: Edward Rosewater, Publisher, June 20, 1893.

Unknown. "Trying Lizzie Borden - The Famous Case Attracts Crowds of Spectators - Sensational Testimony - That Given by the Matron of the Police Station - She Says That Lizzie Told Her Sister That She Had Been Given Away - The Blood-stained Handkerchief Identified," *The Salt Lake Herald*, Salt Lake City, Utah: Herald Company, June 15, 1893.

Unknown. "Lizzie Borden Acquitted - The Jury Return a Finding of Not Guilty - A Wild Scene in Court - The Verdict is Received with Tremendous Cheers by the People," *The Salt Lake Herald*, Salt Lake City, Utah: Herald Company, June 21, 1893.

Unknown. "Lizzie Borden's Trial - The Famous Murder Case Before the Public," *The Daily Herald*, Brownsville, Texas: Jesse O. Wheeler, Publisher, June 9, 1893.

Unknown. "Lizzie Borden's Laughter - What Bridget Sullivan Heard and Saw Before the Murders," *The Sun*, New York, New York: The Sun Printing and Publishing Association, August 27, 1892.

Unknown. "Free From Guilt - Lizzie Borden Acquitted by the Jury - Who Committed the Deed -- Though She is Not the Culprit, Yet is the Mystery No Nearer Solution," *The Morning Call*, San Francisco, California: San Francisco Call Company, June 21, 1893.

Unknown. "The Borden Case. Lawyers Begin Their Arguments - Robinson for the Accused," *The Morning Call*, San Francisco, California: San Francisco Call Company, June 20, 1893.

Unknown. "Summing Up the Case - The Great Borden Murder Trial Nearing the End - Arguments are Begun - Governor Robinson Opens Proceedings with Argument for the Defense - He Rehearses in Chronological Order the Events Connected with the Crime - District Attorney Knowlton Begins His Summing Up," *The Salt Lake Herald*, Salt Lake City, Utah: Herald Company, June 20, 1893.

Unknown. "Lizzie Borden Formerly Charged with Two Murders," *The Daily Herald*, Brownsville, Texas: Jesse O. Wheeler, Publisher, May 12, 1893.

Unknown. "The Borden Murder Case - Bridget Sullivan Finishes Testimony at the Hearing - On Cross-examination She Tells the Same Story as on Direct Examination - Lizzie Borden Came Down the Back Stairs After Her Laughter When Her Father Came In Just Before He Was Killed - Did She See Her Stepmother's Dead Body as She Passed the Spare Room's Door? - An Attempt to Show that Green Pears and Not Poison Caused the Sickness of the Family on the Day Before the Murders," *The Sun*, New York, New York: H. J. Raymond and Company, Publisher, August 28, 1892.

Unknown. "The Borden Murders," *The Daily Herald*, Brownsville, Texas: Jesse O. Wheeler, publisher, August 18, 1892.

Walker, Deward E. *Witchcraft and Sorcery of the American Native Peoples*, Moscow, Idaho: University of Idaho Press, 1989.

Whittier, John Greenleaf. "The Wreck of Rivermouth," *The Complete Poetical Works of John Greenleaf Whittier*, Cambridge, Massachusetts, 1894.

Wiggins, John R. "A Solution to the 1892 Crime? Ruby Cameron Says David Anthony Murdered Lizzie Borden's Parents," *Ellsworth American*, Ellsworth, Maine: Ellsworth American, January 3, 1985.

INDEX